Jack C. Richards & Chuck Sandy

Passages

Third Edition

Workbook 1

CAMBRIDGE
UNIVERSITY PRESS

CAMBRIDGE
UNIVERSITY PRESS

University Printing House, Cambridge CB2 8BS, United Kingdom

One Liberty Plaza, 20th Floor, New York, NY 10006, USA

477 Williamstown Road, Port Melbourne, VIC 3207, Australia

314–321, 3rd Floor, Plot 3, Splendor Forum, Jasola District Centre, New Delhi – 110025, India

79 Anson Road, #06–04/06, Singapore 079906

Cambridge University Press is part of the University of Cambridge.

It furthers the University's mission by disseminating knowledge in the pursuit of education, learning and research at the highest international levels of excellence.

www.cambridge.org
Information on this title: www.cambridge.org/9781107627253

First published 1998
Second edition 2008

20 19 18 17 16 15 14 13 12

Printed in the United Kingdom by Latimer Trend

A catalog record for this publication is available from the British Library

ISBN 978-1-107-62705-5 Student's Book 1
ISBN 978-1-107-62701-7 Student's Book 1A
ISBN 978-1-107-62706-2 Student's Book 1B
ISBN 978-1-107-62725-3 Workbook 1
ISBN 978-1-107-62718-5 Workbook 1A
ISBN 978-1-107-62720-8 Workbook 1B
ISBN 978-1-107-62768-0 Teacher's Edition 1 with Assessment Audio CD/CD-ROM
ISBN 978-1-107-62754-3 Class Audio 1 CDs
ISBN 978-1-107-62769-7 Full Contact 1
ISBN 978-1-107-62771-0 Full Contact 1A
ISBN 978-1-107-62772-7 Full Contact 1B
ISBN 978-1-107-62762-8 DVD 1
ISBN 978-1-107-66626-9 Presentation Plus 1

Additional resources for this publication at www.cambridge.org/passages

Book design: Q2A / Bill Smith
Art direction, layout services and photo research: Tighe Publishing Services

Contents

Credits

Illustration credits

Kim Johnson: 4, 28, 45, 66, 67
Dan McGeehan: 7, 54
Paul Hostetler: 8, 27, 56, 60, 64
Koren Shadmi: 33, 52, 62
James Yamasaki: 22, 35, 61

Photography credits

1 ©Chris Bennett/Aurora/Getty Images; **3** (*clockwise from top center*) ©Keith Levit/Design Pics/Corbis, ©iStock/Thinkstock, ©Iconica/Commercial Eye/Getty Images; **6** ©Barry Austin Photography/Getty Images; **9** ©iStock/Thinkstock; **10** ©dieKleinert/Alamy; **11** ©Holger Hollemann/dpa/picture-alliance/Newscom; **12** ©Christian Guy/Getty Images; **13** ©iStock/Thinkstock; **14** ©iStock/Thinkstock; **15** ©iStock/Thinkstock; **16** ©John W Banagan/Photographer's Choice/Getty Images; **18** (*top left to right*) ©trekandshoot/Shutterstock, ©iStock/Thinkstock, ©iStock.com/wdstock, ©A. T. Willett/Alamy; (*bottom*) ©Rudolf Balasko/Thinkstock; **20** ©Media Bakery; **23** ©Blue Jean Images/Alamy; **24** ©andresrimaging/iStockphoto; **26** ©Pulp Photography/The Image Bank/Getty Images; **29** ©iStock/Thinkstock; **30** ©Clover/SuperStock; **31** ©Eric Isselee/Shutterstock; **34** ©Elke Meitzel/age fotostock; **36** (*top to bottom*) ©assalave/iStockphoto, ©Antonio Balaguer soler/Thinkstock; **38** ©iStock/Thinkstock; **40** ©Wavebreak Media/Thinkstock; **41** ©iStock.com/DSGpro; **44** (*left to right*) ©Jodi/Jake/Media Bakery, ©Masterfile Royalty Free, ©Andresr/age fotostock; **46** ©Caspar Benson/fstop/Corbis; **47** (*left to right*) ©wavebreakmedia/Shutterstock, ©Juanmonino/E+/Getty Images, ©iStock.com/pressureUA, ©homydesign/Shutterstock; **48** (*top*) Janos Levente/Shutterstock, (*center*) Sofi photo/Shutterstock; **49** ©Masterfile Royalty Free; **50** (*clockwise from top left*) Suprijono Suharjoto/Thinkstock, Blend Images/SuperStock, Jack Hollingsworth/Thinkstock, Jupiterimages/Thinkstock; **53** ©Mitchell Funk/Photographer's Choice/Getty Images; **56** ©Stockbyte/Thinkstock; **59** (*left to right*) ©Enrique Algarra/age fotostock, ©Dan Brownsword/Cultura/Getty Images, ©Masterfile Royalty Free; **63** ©Vicki Reid/E+/Getty Images; **68** ©Iakov Kalinin/Shutterstock; **70** Arvind Balaraman/Thinkstock; **71** (*left to right*) ©Greg Epperson/Shutterstock, ©Image Source/age fotostock; **Back cover:** (*clockwise from top*) ©Leszek Bogdewicz/Shutterstock, ©Wavebreak Media/Thinkstock, ©Blend Images/Alamy, ©limpido/Shutterstock

Text credits

The authors and publishers acknowledge the following sources of copyright material and are grateful for the permissions granted. While every effort has been made, it has not always been possible to identify the sources of all the material used, or to trace all copyright holders. If any omissions are brought to our notice, we will be happy to include the appropriate acknowledgments on reprinting.

48 Adapted from "Everyday Creativity," by Carlin Flora, *Psychology Today,* November 1, 2009. Psychology Today © Copyright 2005, www.Psychologytoday.com; **54** Adapted from "Why We Dream: Real Reasons Revealed," by Rachael Rettner, *LiveScience,* June 27, 2010. Reproduced with permission of LiveScience; **60** Adapted from "The Survival Guide for Dealing with Chronic Complainers," by Guy Winch, PhD, *Psychology Today*, July 15, 2011. Reproduced with permission of Guy Winch, www.guywinch.com; **66** Adapted from "Internet On, Inhibitions Off: Why We Tell All," by Matt Ridley, *The Wall Street Journal,* February 18, 2012. Reproduced with permission of The Wall Street Journal. Copyright © 2012 Dow Jones & Company, Inc. All Rights Reserved Worldwide; **72** Adapted from "International Careers: A World of Opportunity: Battling Culture Shock Starts with Trip to Local Bookstores, Seminars: Advance preparation is critical in adjusting to the challenges of life in a foreign country," by Karen E. Klein, *Los Angeles Times*, September 11, 1995. Copyright © 1995. Los Angeles Times. Reprinted with permission.

1 FRIENDS AND FAMILY

LESSON A ▶ *What kind of person are you?*

1 GRAMMAR

Which verbs and expressions can complete the sentences? Write the correct numbers of the sentences next to the verbs.

1. I ________ spending time outdoors.
2. I ________ to spend time outdoors.

a. *1* am afraid of
b. ____ am into
c. ____ avoid
d. ____ can't stand
e. ____ don't mind
f. ____ enjoy
g. ____ feel like
h. ____ hate
i. ____ insist on
j. *1, 2* love
k. ____ prefer
l. ____ worry about

2 GRAMMAR

Read the conversations and complete the sentences using the gerund or infinitive form of the verb. If the two forms are possible, write both of them.

1. Ada: Sam isn't happy when he has nothing to do.
   Gary: I know. It really bothers him.
   Sam can't stand *having nothing to do / to have nothing to do.*
2. Vic: I hardly ever go to school parties anymore.
   Joon: Me neither. They're not as much fun as they used to be.
   Vic and Joon avoid ________________________
3. Tina: You visit your parents on the weekends, don't you?
   Leo: Yes, I visit them on Sundays so I can spend the whole day with them.
   Leo prefers ________________________
4. Tom: Are you going to take an Italian class this summer?
   Ivy: Yes, I am. I love to learn new languages.
   Ivy is into ________________________
5. Ang: Do you want to go rock climbing with me this weekend?
   Sue: I don't know. Rock climbing sounds dangerous!
   Sue is worried about ________________________
6. Josh: What sort of volunteer work do you do for the library, Celia?
   Celia: I love to read to kids, so I volunteer as a storyteller on Saturdays.
   Celia enjoys ________________________

3 GRAMMAR

Write sentences about yourself using the verbs and expressions in the box. Use the gerund of the verbs in the phrases below.

am afraid of	avoid	don't mind	hate	love
am into	can't stand	enjoy	insist on	prefer

1. go shopping on the weekend
   I love going shopping on the weekend.
2. try different types of food
   ____
3. learn new sports or hobbies
   ____
4. meet new people
   ____
5. work on the weekend
   ____
6. clean and organize my room
   ____

4 VOCABULARY

A Match the words to make logical sentences.

1. Angelina volunteers at a hospital. She's very *b*.
2. Stan drives too fast and stays out late. He's _____.
3. Anna never gets angry. She's always _____.
4. Don hates a messy room. He likes being _____.
5. Tad avoids speaking out in class. He's _____.
6. Neil loves throwing parties and making his guests feel welcome. He's _____.
7. City life is crazy! In the country, I feel more _____.
8. Julia insists on doing things her way. She's _____.
9. Mei never hides her true feelings. She's always _____.

a. wild and crazy
b. kind and generous
c. shy and reserved
d. friendly and outgoing
e. calm and cool
f. neat and tidy
g. honest and sincere
h. laid-back and relaxed
i. strong and independent

B Use the vocabulary above to write sentences about people you know.

1. *My sister is shy and reserved. She avoids meeting new people.*
2. ______________________________
3. ______________________________
4. ______________________________
5. ______________________________
6. ______________________________

5 WRITING

A Choose the main idea for each paragraph, and write it in the blank below.

My mother loves speaking Chinese.

My mother is very adventurous.

I really admire my mother.

I am not like my mother at all.

1. ______________________. She enjoys doing unusual things and pushing herself to the limit. Last year, for example, she insisted on visiting China. She enrolled in Chinese language classes, planned her trip, and then took off across China with a friend. She loves exploring new places, and she doesn't hesitate to start conversations with locals wherever she goes.

I have a friend named John.

My friend John and I are in the same class.

My friend John is the kind of person who loves to talk.

My friend John always says what is on his mind.

2. ______________________. He's probably the most outspoken person I know. Last week after class, for example, he said to our English teacher, "Some of the students are a little confused by this week's class, but I have some ideas to help explain it to them. Do you want to hear my suggestions?" John was saying what he thought, and luckily our teacher was willing to listen to him.

B Complete these two sentences. Then choose one of them, and write a paragraph to support it.

1. My friend ______________ is the kind of person who ______________

   ____

2. ______________ is the most ______________ person I know.

   ____

   ____

   ____

   ____

   ____

   ____

LESSON B ► *Every family is different.*

1 GRAMMAR

Read the blog entry. Then underline the noun clauses.

May 15, 2014

I love my family so much, and I really get along with everyone – my parents and my four brothers and sisters. However, sometimes they drive me crazy. There are both good and bad things about coming from a large family. One of the best things about coming from a large family is that I always have someone to talk to. Unfortunately, one of the disadvantages is that I never have any privacy. And of course, the trouble with not having any privacy is that I never have any space I can call my own. Our house is big, but sometimes not big enough!

2 GRAMMAR

Combine each pair of sentences into one sentence using noun clauses.

1. I'm the youngest in my family. The best thing is I'm the center of attention.
   The best thing about being the youngest is that I'm the center of attention.
2. I have a lot of kids. The disadvantage is I can't give each of them the individual attention they want.
   ____
   ____
3. I live with my father-in-law. The problem is we disagree about everything.
   ____
   ____
4. I have two younger sisters. The worst thing is they always want to know all about my personal life.
   ____
   ____
5. I have an identical twin. The trouble is no one can ever tell us apart.
   ____
   ____

3 GRAMMAR

Use noun clauses and your own ideas to complete these sentences.

1. A disadvantage of having siblings who are successful is *that my parents expect me to be successful, too.*
2. The problem with having a large family is ______________________________
3. The best thing about having grandparents is ______________________________
4. The trouble with being part of a two-income family is ______________________________
5. One benefit of living far away from your family is ______________________________
6. The worst thing about taking a family vacation is ______________________________
7. An advantage of living with siblings is ______________________________

4 VOCABULARY

Are the statements true or false? Choose the correct answer.

	True	False
Sylvia's mother has a great-uncle named Martin.		
1. Sylvia is Martin's great-granddaughter.	☐	☑
2. Sylvia's mother is Martin's grandniece.	☐	☐
Hal's wife, Nikki, has a sister named Joanne.		
3. Joanne is Hal's sister-in-law.	☐	☐
4. Joanne is Hal's grandmother.	☐	☐
Hugo's niece Diana has a son-in-law named Jason.		
5. Jason's wife is Hugo's granddaughter.	☐	☐
6. Diana is Jason's mother-in-law.	☐	☐
Molly's nephew Tom has a daughter named Jennifer.		
7. Molly is Tom's aunt.	☐	☐
8. Molly is Jennifer's great-aunt.	☐	☐
Irene's father, Roberto, has a grandfather named Eduardo.		
9. Eduardo is Roberto's grandson.	☐	☐
10. Eduardo is Irene's great-grandfather.	☐	☐

5 READING

A Read the article. Then choose the main idea of each paragraph.

Is it Better or Worse to Be an Only Child?

If you are an only child – someone with no brothers or sisters – you have probably been the object of both sympathy and suspicion. "Oh, you poor thing!" some people say. "You must have been so lonely!" Other people might not say much, but you know they are thinking that you are selfish, spoiled, and have no idea how to get along with others. People assume that only children are somehow at a disadvantage because of their lack of siblings, and this idea has probably been around as long as only children have.

Recent studies, however, have shown that the stereotype of the only child is really just a myth. Only children show very little difference from children with siblings, and as adults they are just as likely to be well adjusted. One slight difference they show from children with multiple siblings is that they often score higher on intelligence and achievement tests. But first-born children and those with only one sibling have similar results, so we can't really say this is a characteristic of the only child, either. The one undeniable difference is that only children get more of their parents' time and attention for the simple reason that there are fewer demands on the parents. The same goes for educational opportunities – there tend to be more resources available in single-child households. However, there is little evidence that this has long-term benefits for only children.

For some reason, though, popular opinion and culture seem to have a hard time accepting the fact that only children are just like everyone else. Movies and TV shows still portray "onlies" as socially awkward and expecting to get whatever they ask for. What keeps the stereotype alive? Could it be that most of us have wished – at one point or another – to be an only child? At least we wouldn't have had to deal with siblings playing with our toys, borrowing our clothes, and eating that last piece of cake we had saved for later.

1. First paragraph:
   - ☐ a. Only children all wish they had siblings.
   - ☐ b. Only children think other children are selfish.
   - ☐ c. Many people make assumptions about only children.

2. Second paragraph:
   - ☐ a. Only children really are different from children with siblings.
   - ☐ b. Only children are basically the same as those with siblings.
   - ☐ c. No one has really studied only children.

3. Third paragraph:
   - ☐ a. The popular view of only children seems difficult to change.
   - ☐ b. The popular view of only children has changed recently.
   - ☐ c. The popular view of only children is based on facts.

B Are the statements true or false? Choose the correct answer. Then rewrite the false statements to make them true.

	True	False
1. Some people feel sorry for only children.	☐	☐
2. When only children grow up, they are less sociable than children with siblings.	☐	☐
3. Only children are more intelligent than children with siblings.	☐	☐
4. According to the author, people's ideas about only children need to change.	☐	☐

2 MISTAKES AND MYSTERIES

LESSON A ▶ *Life lessons*

1 VOCABULARY

Correct the underlined mistakes in each sentence. Write the correct form of a verb from the box after each sentence. Sometimes more than one answer is possible.

aggravate	avoid	cause	deal with	identify	ignore	run into	solve

1. Jim said I solved the problem with my tablet when I spilled water on it. *caused*
2. Grace didn't pay her credit card bill last month. When she didn't pay it again this month, she only ran into her debt problem. ____________
3. I always ask Kate for help with math. She can ignore any problem. ____________
4. Tim's report was late. He aggravated problems with his computer that he didn't expect. ____________
5. John caused his weight problem for years. Now he can't fit into any of his clothes! ____________
6. Mike has many problems with his projects at work, so he often stays late to identify them. ____________
7. My brother is an amazing auto mechanic. He can look at a car's engine and ignore what is causing problems. ____________
8. Pedro identifies problems with computer viruses by updating his antivirus software every week. ____________

2 GRAMMAR

Choose the past modal or phrasal modal of obligation that best completes each sentence.

1. I *wasn't supposed to* / *had to* (circled) give Mr. Lee my phone when he caught me texting in class.
2. Eve was worried that she *needed to* / *didn't have to* pass her exam to graduate.
3. Frank *didn't have to* / *was supposed to* take his grandmother to the store, but he wanted to.
4. I *needed to buy* / *shouldn't have bought* these boots, but they were on sale!
5. Bob *was supposed to* / *didn't need to* bring dessert to the party, but he brought an appetizer instead.
6. I *didn't need to* / *was supposed to* clean my apartment before my friend arrived, but I didn't have time.

3 GRAMMAR

Complete the email with the past modals and phrasal modals of obligation in the box. Use each modal only once.

didn't have to	had to	needed to	should have	shouldn't have	was supposed to

New Message

Hey Ally,

I (1) *was supposed to* pick up my brother at practice yesterday, but I forgot. Well, I didn't forget . . . I went to the café instead. I (2) ________________ go, but I wanted to see you guys. I (3) ________________ thought about my brother, but I didn't. When my mom discovered that my brother (4) ________________ walk home alone, she got upset with me. She said I (5) ________________ forgotten about my brother. So now she doesn't trust me. She said I (6) ________________ think about my responsibilities and behave more responsibly to regain her trust. Anyway, this means I won't be able to go on the trip with you guys this weekend. I'm so frustrated!

Gigi

4 GRAMMAR

Use past modals and phrasal modals of obligation to write a sentence for each situation.

1. make a left turn instead of a right turn

I should have made a left turn instead of a right turn.

2. hand in a research paper today

____

3. pick up a friend from the airport

____

4. not eat a big lunch

____

5 WRITING

A Look at the brainstorming notes and add two more ideas to each category.

Apologizing for being late to an appointment

Do	*Don't*
• *let the person know why you're late*	• *make excuses*
• *be sincere*	• *be disrespectful*
• *take responsibility for your lateness*	• *be overly apologetic*
• ______________________	• ______________________
• ______________________	• ______________________

B Complete the sentences with ideas from your brainstorming notes.

1. You need to ______________________ when you apologize.
2. You shouldn't ______________________ when you apologize.

C Choose one of the sentences you completed above and brainstorm supporting ideas for its topic. Then write a paragraph based on your brainstorming notes.

You shouldn't make excuses when you apologize. You have to simply say you are sorry. For example, if you are late for an appointment, you should never say you were confused about the meeting time. Next, you shouldn't say your directions were bad. In addition, you shouldn't blame public transportation for your lateness. . . .

____

____

____

____

____

____

____

____

____

____

____

____

LESSON B ► *I can't explain it!*

1 GRAMMAR

Underline the modals in the sentences. Then write *C* for modals expressing degrees of certainty or *O* for modals expressing obligation, advice, or opinion.

__C__ 1. Some people are certain the boats and airplanes that have disappeared in the Bermuda Triangle must have vanished due to human error.

_____ 2. Others believe the boats and airplanes that disappeared in the Bermuda Triangle could have been affected by supernatural forces.

_____ 3. The people who vanished should have planned their route more carefully to avoid entering the Bermuda Triangle.

_____ 4. Experts say the people who got lost in the Bermuda Triangle must not have been prepared for strong water currents and changing weather patterns.

_____ 5. While many people have successfully navigated through the Bermuda Triangle, there are others who shouldn't have tried, as they are now missing.

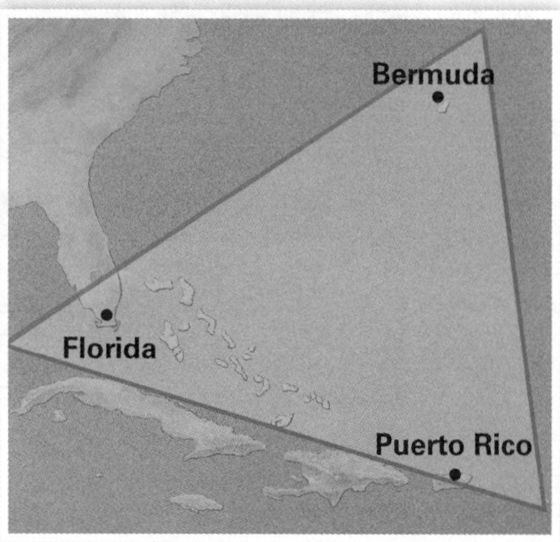

2 GRAMMAR

Choose the phrase that best completes each sentence.

THE BLOG SPACE

August 31

I just watched a documentary about the princess who died in a mysterious car accident. It was so interesting – everyone (1) *should watch* / *should have been watching* it. The princess was too young and smart to die in such an awful accident. Many people feel that she (2) *shouldn't have gone* / *may not have been going* in the car that night. Anyway, the documentary said there are many theories about how the car accident happened. Some people think the car's brakes (3) *might have been tampered* / *should have tampered* with. Others believe that the princess's driver (4) *should have caused* / *could have caused* the accident. Some even think the princess (5) *could have been kidnapped* / *could have kidnapped.* The police never figured out what really happened. I'm not sure what to believe, but there (6) *shouldn't have been* / *must have been* a way to solve this mystery!

Comments (4)

3 GRAMMAR

Use modals expressing degrees of certainty and your own ideas to write about the following situations.

1. Your friend got the highest grade on a difficult English exam.
   He must have studied really hard. It's also possible the test may have been too easy.
   ____
2. You don't hear from your best friend for several days.
   ____
   ____
3. Your favorite jacket isn't in your closet.
   ____
   ____
4. You see some very large footprints while walking in the park.
   ____
   ____

4 VOCABULARY

Use the verbs of belief in the box to write a sentence about each topic.

assume	be sure	figure	know for a fact
be certain	bet	guess	suppose
be positive	doubt	have a hunch	suspect

1. Elephants are the world's smartest animals.
   I am sure that elephants are the world's smartest animals.
2. There is a monster that lives in Loch Ness in Scotland.
   ____
   ____
3. Global warming is causing changes in worldwide weather patterns.
   ____
4. People eat bananas more than any other fruit in the world.
   ____
5. Some pyramids were built more than 2,000 years ago.
   ____
6. Dinosaurs were wiped out by an asteroid that caused changes in the climate.
   ____

5 READING

A Read the article quickly to find the answers to the questions.

1. When did the British couple go on vacation? ___________________
2. Who gave the couple directions to Spain? ___________________

Hotel Time Warp

The idea of traveling backward or forward through time has long been a favorite subject of books, movies, and TV shows. Although some scientists suspect that it may actually be possible, no one has invented a way to make it happen. However, many people have reported traveling in time.

One famous story is about a British couple who were vacationing in France in 1979. They were looking for a place to stay for the night and noticed a sign for an old circus. They found a hotel nearby and discovered that almost everything inside the hotel was made of heavy wood and there were no modern conveniences such as telephones or TVs. Furthermore, their room doors did not have locks, and the windows had wooden shutters instead of glass. In the morning, two police officers entered the hotel wearing old-fashioned uniforms with capes. After getting confusing directions from the officers to Spain, the couple paid their amazingly inexpensive hotel bill and left.

Two weeks later, the couple returned to France and decided to stay at the odd, but very cheap, hotel again. This time, however, the hotel was nowhere to be found. Positive that they were in the exact same spot because of the circus posters, the couple realized that the hotel had completely vanished. Even more confusing, they found that the photographs they had taken inside the hotel did not develop. Later, their research uncovered that the French officers had been wearing uniforms dating from before 1905.

Researchers analyzing these events call them "time slips" and believe that they must happen randomly and spontaneously. However, researchers cannot explain why, when, or how they occur. But when they do occur, people are so bewildered and confused that they can barely explain what happened to them, even though they are sure they have experienced some sort of time travel.

B Read the article again. Choose the statements you think the author would agree with.

☐ 1. Time travel is not a favorite subject of books, movies, and television shows.
☐ 2. Few people have reported traveling through time.
☐ 3. Scientists have invented a way to make time travel happen.
☐ 4. People who experience time slips do not remember the experience afterwards.
☐ 5. It is not known why, when, or how time slips occur.
☐ 6. Many people believe they have traveled through time.

3 EXPLORING NEW CITIES

LESSON A ▶ *Popular destinations*

1 GRAMMAR

Underline the relative clauses in the postcard. Then add commas where necessary.

July 15

Dear Mom and Dad,

Greetings from Maine where the water is too cold for us to go swimming, but the scenery is beautiful. We're having a great time, and we've enjoyed every place that we've visited. This week we're in Bar Harbor which is a lovely island town. The place is absolutely full of tourists! Tonight we're going for a ride on a boat that will take us to one of the nearby islands. Our friend James who lives here has already taken us hiking and to the Bar Harbor Music Festival. It's been fun! That's it for now. We miss you.

Love, Sara and Eric

2 GRAMMAR

Join the following sentences using non-defining relative clauses.

1. Many tourists enjoy seeing the Kuala Lumpur skyline in Malaysia. It includes some of the tallest skyscrapers in the world.
   Many tourists enjoy seeing the Kuala Lumpur skyline in Malaysia, which includes some of the tallest skyscrapers in the world.
2. People visit Washington, D.C., in the spring. They can see the cherry trees in bloom then.
   ____
3. The cherry trees in Washington, D.C., were a gift from the Japanese government to the U.S. They are admired by everyone.
   ____
4. Thousands of years ago, people in Mexico began to grow corn. Corn continues to be a very important food in Mexico today.
   ____
5. The tortilla is typically eaten in Mexico. It is a thin, flat bread.
   ____

3 VOCABULARY

Choose the correct words to complete the sentences.

1. When preparing to host the 2012 Olympics, London updated its *hotels / climate / transportation system* with improvements to its subway.
2. New York City has hundreds of restaurants offering a wide variety of *climates / cuisines / green spaces*, including Italian, Chinese, and Indian.
3. Many people are moving from bigger cities to smaller towns because the *cost of living / landmark / climate* is more affordable.
4. If you enjoy *neighborhoods / shopping / nightlife*, you'll love the music and live shows in Rio de Janeiro.
5. Some people think Reykjavik, Iceland, is cold in the wintertime, but surprisingly, it has a very mild *climate / cuisine / transportation system* during the winter months.
6. Some famous *green spaces / neighborhoods / landmarks* in Paris include the Eiffel Tower and the Louvre Museum.
7. Many cities are preserving *green spaces / hotels / cuisines* in their downtown areas for people to have picnics, walk their dogs, and enjoy outdoor concerts.

4 GRAMMAR

Use defining or non-defining relative clauses to write sentences about these topics.

- a popular tourist activity in your city
- a town with many historical attractions
- a place with a good climate
- an excellent city for shopping

1. *Tourists in Rome like to visit the famous squares, which have many beautiful statues and fountains.*
2. ______
3. ______
4. ______

5 WRITING

A Look at the words and phrases in the box about Chiang Mai, Thailand. Choose the main idea and write it in the center of the mind map. Then write the supporting details in the mind map.

reasonable prices	clothing
fruits and spices	handicrafts
a wonderful night market	jewelry

B Now read the paragraph about Chiang Mai. Answer the questions.

> Chiang Mai is a city in northern Thailand that has a wonderful night market. In the evening, the main street is lined with small stands and shops that sell almost anything you can imagine. Some stands sell jewelry or clothing, others sell traditional Thai handicrafts, and still others sell fresh fruit and spices. I love spicy Thai food. It's easy to spend an entire evening just looking at everything. If you decide to buy something, you won't be disappointed. The prices are very reasonable. There are a lot of wonderful attractions in Chiang Mai, but the night market is a favorite for many people.

1. What is this paragraph about? ______________________________
2. What is the topic sentence of the paragraph? ______________________________

   ____
3. Which sentence does not support the main idea? Cross it out.

C Write a paragraph about one of the places you mentioned in Exercise 4 on page 14. Include a topic sentence with the main idea and several supporting ideas.

____

____

____

____

____

LESSON B ► *My kind of town*

1 GRAMMAR

Unscramble the words to complete the sentences about these cities.

1. a / with fascinating buildings / city / coastal / charming
   Salvador is *a charming coastal city with fascinating buildings.*
2. a / European / city / quaint / old / with a lovely castle
   Prague is ______________________________
3. a / lively / city / with huge skyscrapers / modern
   Taipei is ______________________________
4. a / dynamic / port / with trendy shopping malls / city
   Singapore is ______________________________
5. a / industrial / modern / large / city / with a beautiful lakeshore
   Chicago is ______________________________
6. an / with world-famous theme parks / tourist / exciting / destination
   Orlando is ______________________________

2 VOCABULARY

Choose the word that best completes each sentence.

border coastal college mountain port rural tourist

1. Ana lives in a *rural* town. The nearest big city is more than two hours away.
2. The local university employs most of the people living in this ____________ town.
3. ____________ towns are near an ocean, a lake, or a river where ships unload cargo.
4. People traveling from the U.S. to Mexico through ____________ towns must stop and show their passports or other identification.
5. I work in a small ____________ town with great beaches and seafood places.
6. We stopped in a crowded ____________ town full of overpriced souvenir shops.
7. Nick lives in a ____________ town that is nearly 3,000 meters above sea level.

3 GRAMMAR

Rewrite the sentences using the words in parentheses.

1. The streets are well lit, but it's best to be careful at night. (in spite of)
   In spite of the well-lit streets, it's best to be careful at night.
2. There is a crime problem, but it's still a wonderful place to visit. (despite)
   ____
3. The shopping malls are crowded, but people aren't buying much. (although)
   ____
4. It snows a lot, but I still like living here. (even though)
   ____
5. My city is on the ocean, but the water here is too polluted for people to go swimming. (however)
   ____
6. The city center is very picturesque, but there's not much to do. (nevertheless)
   ____
7. There's a lot to do here at night, but it's a very noisy neighborhood. (on the other hand)
   ____

4 GRAMMAR

Complete the sentences with your own opinions about cities you know.

1. The worst thing about *Los Angeles* is *the heavy traffic*.
   In spite of that, *it is an ideal place to live*.
2. The worst thing about __________ is __________.
   Nevertheless, ______________________________.
3. The best thing about __________ is __________.
   However, ______________________________.
4. Even though __________ has a lot of __________,
   ______________________________.
5. The weather in __________ is __________.
   On the other hand, ______________________________.
6. __________ would be a great place to live. However, __________
   ______________________________.
7. Although __________ is a favorite tourist destination for many, it also has its problems. For example, ______________________________.

5 READING

A Match the words in the box with the photos. Then read two articles about megacities.

auto emissions **carpooling** **a landfill** **public transportation**

1. *carpooling* 2. ______ 3. ______ 4. ______

MEGACITIES: TWO VIEWS

1 The world's population is not only growing, it is also becoming more urbanized. An increasing number of people are moving to cities in the hope of having a better life. The cities promise steady work and higher salaries. With more money, people think they can provide for their families more easily.

As the population becomes more urbanized, megacities are created. Yes, there are more jobs in urban areas, but is the quality of life better in these megacities? A quick survey of several major cities reveals some of their problems: Pollution from auto emissions is poisoning the air; landfills are overflowing with garbage. With declining resources and growing competition, sometimes there is not enough food. These are all very serious problems.

We cannot get rid of megacities – they are here to stay. What we should concentrate on, however, is building "villages" inside the cities. These "urban villages" could be self-sufficient and grow their own food. The members of these villages would recycle more and do less damage to the environment. The villages would serve the needs of the local people, not big business. We need to limit large-scale development, not encourage it.

megacity a city with a population of 10 million or more

2 It's true that megacities have problems, but these have been exaggerated. The truth of the matter is that people move to cities to escape their hard life in the country. Urban areas, even with their problems, offer people a better life than rural areas. The old ways of life in rural areas have broken down, and it is now very difficult to make a living as a farmer.

People live longer in the cities. Medical care is better. And, of course, employment opportunities can be found more easily in the city. We should continue to develop city services so that people can enjoy their lives in the world's urban centers.

Rather than limiting development, we should encourage it. Public transportation systems need to be developed so that people can travel to and from work and school easily. Carpooling should be encouraged to cut down on pollution. The more we clean up and develop our megacities, the more life will improve for the residents.

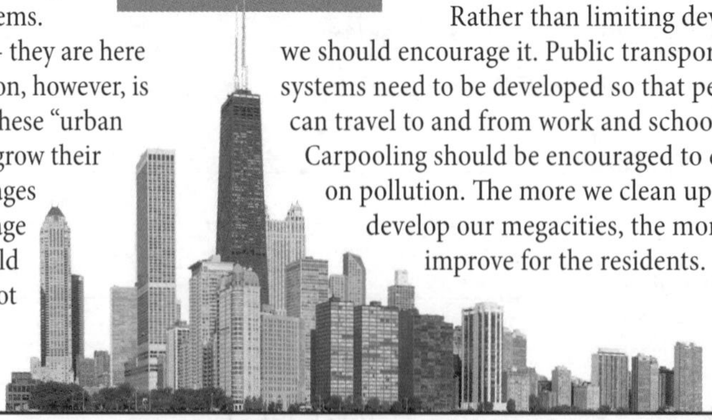

B Match the statements with the articles that support them.

	1	2	1 & 2
1. "Megacities have problems."	☐	☐	☐
2. "Life in rural areas is hard."	☐	☐	☐
3. "We should recreate village life in the cities."	☐	☐	☐
4. "There are more chances to work in the cities."	☐	☐	☐
5. "Continued development will hurt the quality of life."	☐	☐	☐
6. "Continued development can improve the quality of life."	☐	☐	☐

4 EARLY BIRDS AND NIGHT OWLS

LESSON A ▶ *It's about time!*

1 GRAMMAR

Combine the sentences using the words in parentheses. Use reduced time clauses wherever possible.

1. Classes are over for the day. I often go out with my friends. (after)
   After classes are over for the day, I often go out with my friends.
2. I lost my watch. I've been late for all my appointments. (ever since)
   ______
3. You should relax and count to 10. You start to feel stressed. (as soon as)
   ______
4. I go for a run. I stretch for at least 15 minutes. (right before)
   ______
5. She shouldn't listen to music. She is studying for a big test. (while)
   ______
6. I watch TV. I fall asleep. (until)
   ______
7. I get to the office. I start planning what I need to do that day. (from the moment)
   ______

2 GRAMMAR

Read the statements. Are they true for you? Choose true or false. Then rewrite the false statements to make them true.

	True	False
1. Whenever I get stressed out, I take a walk and try to relax. *I usually eat a lot of snacks whenever I get stressed out.*	☐	☑
2. As soon as I wake up, I check my email and phone messages. ______	☐	☐
3. Ever since I started studying English, I've spoken more confidently. ______	☐	☐
4. I like to read the news while I'm eating lunch. ______	☐	☐
5. After I fall asleep, nothing can wake me up. ______	☐	☐

3 VOCABULARY

Use the phrasal verbs from the box to complete the conversations.

burn out
calm down
chill out
doze off
perk up
turn in

1. A: I lost my car keys! I'm going to be late for my doctor's appointment!
   B: You need to *calm down*. Relax. Maybe you can reschedule.
2. A: You look tired. You need to ____________ before our meeting.
   B: Yeah, you're right. Maybe I should have a cup of coffee.
3. A: Poor Jenny. She has two papers to write and a final exam to study for.
   B: That's a lot of work. I hope she doesn't ____________ before graduation.
4. A: My flight leaves tomorrow morning at six o'clock.
   B: You should ____________ early tonight so you'll wake up on time.
5. A: What a day! I had three meetings and a business lunch. I'm so tired.
   B: Let's have some dinner. Then let's ____________ and watch TV.
6. A: Oh, sorry! I guess I fell asleep.
   B: You should go to bed earlier. Then you wouldn't ____________ in class.

4 GRAMMAR

Use time clauses to complete the sentences so they are true for you.

1. *As soon as* I get home from work, I *change into some comfortable clothes and make dinner.*
2. ____________ I have the chance to chill out, I ____________
3. ____________ I met my best friend, we ____________
4. ____________ I started riding a bike, I ____________
5. ____________ eating a large meal, I ____________

5 WRITING

A Read the paragraph and choose the best topic sentence. Is each topic sentence too general, too specific, or just right? Choose the correct answer.

1. ______________________________

We experience a gradual rise of energy in the morning, peaking around noon. There is a slow decline in energy in the midafternoon with a second peak early in the evening. This is followed by a steady decline in energy until bedtime. Everyone experiences these energy patterns. They are a part of daily life.

	Too general	Too specific	Just right
a. People need energy to get through the day.	☐	☐	☐
b. People's energy patterns change according to the time of day.	☐	☐	☐
c. Everyone's energy peaks around noon.	☐	☐	☐

2. ______________________________

Newborn babies sleep an average of 15 to 18 hours a day, but as children grow older, they sleep less. However, as teenagers, they seem to need a lot of sleep again. It is not unusual for teens to sleep until noon on weekends if their parents let them. As people age beyond their thirties, they tend to sleep less and less and for shorter periods of time.

	Too general	Too specific	Just right
a. People's sleep needs change as they go through life.	☐	☐	☐
b. Babies sleep more than elderly people.	☐	☐	☐
c. Everyone needs sleep.	☐	☐	☐

3. ______________________________

In fact, Americans now spend close to $30 billion a year on vitamins and food supplements. Vitamin companies supply an almost endless variety of vitamins. There are multivitamins for adults, special vitamins for women, flavored vitamins for children, and even vitamins to help students study better. New types of vitamins come out regularly, and at least one store in every shopping mall sells vitamins.

	Too general	Too specific	Just right
a. Vitamins supplement a healthy diet.	☐	☐	☐
b. Vitamins are popular with women.	☐	☐	☐
c. In the U.S., vitamins are big business.	☐	☐	☐

B Write a topic sentence about how to keep your energy up or sleep well. Then write a paragraph that supports your main idea.

____

____

1 VOCABULARY

Rewrite the sentences by replacing the underlined words with phrases from the box. Sometimes more than one answer is possible.

be fast asleep
be sound asleep
be wide awake
drift off
feel drowsy
have a sleepless night
nod off
sleep like a log
take a power nap
toss and turn

1. If Elisa is worried when she goes to bed, she is unable to sleep.
   If Elisa is worried when she goes to bed, she tosses and turns.
   If Elisa is worried when she goes to bed, she has a sleepless night.
2. My father always falls asleep after eating a heavy meal.
   ____
3. Simon often sleeps for a few minutes to boost his creativity at work.
   ____
4. The loud music didn't wake Sue. She must be in a deep sleep.
   ____
5. Liz is lucky she sleeps heavily because her roommate snores so loudly!
   ____
6. Marina isn't tired at all. In fact, she is completely alert!
   ____
7. Kenji often begins to feel sleepy when he reads on the train or in a car.
   ____

2 GRAMMAR

Choose the word or phrase that best completes each sentence.

1. *Considering that / Just in case / (Unless)* I'm really worried, I usually sleep well.
2. *Even if / Just in case / Only if* I have bad dreams, I don't recall the details later.
3. *Even if / As long as / Unless* I sleep well, I wake up feeling rested.
4. *Considering that / Only if / Unless* I didn't sleep last night, I feel pretty good.
5. Bring an umbrella with you *only if / as long as / just in case* it rains later.

3 GRAMMAR

Use the information in the box and the expressions in parentheses to write new sentences.

I drink too much caffeine during the day.
I forget to set my alarm clock.
I get thirsty in the middle of the night.
I sleep deeply.
I'm completely exhausted.
I've slept well the night before.

1. I always feel great in the morning. (as long as)
   I always feel great in the morning as long as I've slept well the night before.
2. Sometimes I have trouble drifting off. (even if)
   ____
3. My neighbors listen to loud music every night. (considering that)
   ____
4. I never oversleep in the morning. (unless)
   ____
5. I keep a glass of water by my bed. (just in case)
   ____
6. I have trouble falling asleep. (only . . . if)
   ____

4 GRAMMAR

Answer these questions using clauses with *as long as, considering that, even if, (just) in case, only . . . if,* or *unless.*

1. Do you stay awake thinking, or do you fall asleep as soon as you lie down?
   I only stay awake thinking if I'm having a problem at work.
2. Are you usually alert or still sleepy when you first get up in the morning?
   ____
3. Do you ever take naps during the day, or do you wait until bedtime to sleep?
   ____
4. Do you sleep like a log all night, or do you toss and turn?
   ____
5. Do you always need eight hours of sleep a night, or can you survive on less?
   ____

5 READING

A Read the article quickly. Which three sleep theories are mentioned?

____

Why Sleep?

For some people, sleep is a great pleasure that they look forward to after a long day. For others, sleep is just a necessity, almost a waste of time. Regardless of where you stand, there's no denying that, at some point, everyone needs sleep. Without it, you'll find yourself irritable, confused, and lacking in energy. And the fact is that humans can survive longer without food than they can without sleep. But why is sleep necessary?

There are several theories that try to explain why sleep is so important. One of them, the energy conservation theory, suggests that a period of inactivity gives the body a chance to save energy. Basically, most mammals sleep through the night because instinct tells them it is less practical and more dangerous to hunt for or gather food in the dark. Another possible explanation is the restorative theory. According to this theory, the body needs time to repair itself after the physical efforts of the day, and certain repair functions can only happen during sleep.

One of the most fascinating discoveries about sleep is that it is not a period of total inactivity, as scientists previously believed. While we sleep, things are happening in the brain that researchers are only beginning to understand. The brain plasticity theory states that sleep is necessary to allow the brain to adjust to new experiences and information, and that a reorganization of the information in the brain takes place during sleep. Experts say that plenty of sleep the first night after learning a new skill or a new set of facts is crucial for improving memory and performance.

Dr. Robert Stickgold, a cognitive neuroscientist, says, "There's an old joke that the function of sleep is to cure sleepiness." Since there is no real agreement on a single reason for sleep, that may be the best explanation we have. Not to mention the fact that, after an exhausting day, it just feels good.

B Are the statements true or false? Choose the correct answer. Then rewrite the false statements to make them true.

	True	False
1. Humans need food more than they need sleep.	☐	☐
2. The conservation and restorative theories are concerned more with physical than mental processes.	☐	☐
3. Scientists have always believed there is brain activity during sleep.	☐	☐
4. Scientists have a complete understanding of what happens in the brain during sleep.	☐	☐
5. According to the brain plasticity theory, sleeping well after learning something new will help you remember it.	☐	☐

5 COMMUNICATION

LESSON A ▶ *Making conversation*

1 GRAMMAR

Are these customs similar to or different from customs in your culture? Choose your answer. For the customs that are different, write an explanation.

	Similar	Different
1. It's customary in India to take your shoes off when entering a home.	☐	☐
In my culture, ______________________		
______________________		
2. In Greece, it's not unusual to kiss friends and relatives on both cheeks when meeting them.	☐	☐
______________________		
______________________		
3. In some countries, owning a pet like a dog, a cat, or a bird is considered inappropriate.	☐	☐
______________________		
______________________		
4. In the U.S., arriving 30 minutes early to a dinner party isn't a good idea.	☐	☐
______________________		
______________________		

2 VOCABULARY

Choose the word or phrase that best describes how each situation is viewed in your culture. Then write a sentence about the custom.

1. saying hello to strangers (appropriate / inappropriate / (normal))
   Saying hello to strangers in my culture is considered normal.
2. opening a door for someone (bad form / polite / strange)
   ____
3. splitting a restaurant bill with a friend (a compliment / an insult / typical)
   ____
4. offering your seat on a bus to a child (normal / offensive / unusual)
   ____
5. chewing with your mouth open (polite / rude / typical)
   ____

3 GRAMMAR

Use the information in the chart to make sentences about the dos and don'ts of customs in the U.S. Use the infinitive form of the verb in your answers.

Customs in the U.S.	
Dos	**Don'ts**
Acceptable: Use hand gestures while speaking.	Inappropriate: Talk about religion or politics.
Not unusual: Ask people how they feel.	Not a good idea: Ask about someone's salary.
Customary: Ask what someone does for a living.	Rude: Tell someone he or she has gained weight.

1. *It's acceptable to use hand gestures while speaking.*
2. ______
3. ______
4. ______
5. ______
6. ______

4 GRAMMAR

Use gerunds to rewrite the sentences you wrote above.

1. *Using hand gestures while speaking is acceptable.*
2. ______
3. ______
4. ______
5. ______
6. ______

5 GRAMMAR

What should people know about your customs? Write sentences with infinitive phrases or gerunds.

1. meeting business associates
When you meet business associates in my culture, it's typical to exchange business cards.
When you meet business associates in my culture, exchanging business cards is typical.

2. getting married
______

3. eating out ______

6 WRITING

A Read the parts of a paragraph about small talk. They have been mixed up. Put them in the correct order according to the outline.

1. ______ Topic sentence
2. ______ Supporting sentences: General example
3. ______ Supporting sentences: Personal example
4. ______ Concluding sentence

a For example, personal income is seen as too private to be a suitable topic for small talk in the U.S. People in the U.S. normally avoid asking other people how much they make, and they rarely offer information about their own salary.

b Small talk is common in every culture, but the topics that are considered suitable or unsuitable vary from country to country.

c In conclusion, when dealing with people from other cultures, it's a good idea to be aware of which topics are considered suitable and avoid those that aren't – in that way, you can avoid creating the kind of awkwardness that small talk is meant to reduce.

d I remember being very taken aback when, at a party, a person from another country asked me what I did for a living and then asked me how much money I made. My inability to answer right away made me realize that this really is a taboo topic in our culture, if not in others. After some hesitation, and hoping I didn't sound rude, my answer was, "Oh, enough to support myself."

B Think of a topic of small talk that is avoided in your country or a country you know well. Write notes for a short paragraph about the topic using the outline below.

1. Topic sentence: ______________________________
2. Supporting sentences:
   - 2.1 General example: ______________________________
   - 2.2 Personal example: ______________________________
3. Concluding sentence: ______________________________

C Write a paragraph about the topic using the outline and your notes above.

____

____

____

____

____

____

____

LESSON B ► *It's personal.*

1 GRAMMAR

Read Victoria and Alicia's conversation about a movie star. Then read the sentences below. One mistake is underlined in each sentence. Rewrite the sentences with the correct verb tenses.

Victoria: Did you see the new *Star Monthly*? Jenny Roberts bought an amazing new house!
Alicia: When did she buy it?
Victoria: She moved in last week.
Alicia: Lucky Jenny. Is she happy?
Victoria: Actually, she's not. That's what it says here in *Star Monthly*.
Alicia: Really? Let me see that.
Victoria: Yeah. She found out the closets are too small!

1. Victoria told Alicia that Jenny Roberts did buy a new house.
   Victoria told Alicia that Jenny Roberts had bought a new house.
2. Alicia asked Victoria when she was buying it.
   ____
3. Victoria told Alicia that she was moving in last week.
   ____
4. Alicia asked Victoria if Jenny is happy.
   ____
5. Victoria told Alicia that Jenny will not be happy.
   ____
6. Victoria told Alicia that Jenny has found out the closets were too small.
   ____

2 GRAMMAR

Read the conversation. Use reported speech to complete the sentences.

Mark: Sandra, sit down. Did you hear about Paul Alvaro?

Sandra: No, I didn't. What happened?

Mark: He got a promotion.

Sandra: When did it happen?

Mark: Yesterday. The official announcement will be made soon.

1. Mark told Sandra *to sit down.*
2. He asked her ______________________
3. She said that ______________________
4. She asked Mark ______________________
5. Mark said that Paul ______________________
6. Sandra asked Mark ______________________
7. Mark said that it ______________________
8. He said that the official announcement ______________________

3 VOCABULARY

Use the expressions in the box to complete the blog entry. Sometimes more than one answer is possible.

she claimed that	she explained that	she warned me not to
she encouraged me to	she told us that	she wondered

November 10

My technology teacher gave us a difficult assignment today. (1) *She told us that* we had to prepare a 10-minute oral presentation for Friday. I can't stand speaking in front of the class. Anyway, I asked my teacher if I could do a different assignment – like a written report. (2) ______________ why I didn't want to do the presentation, so I told her how nervous I get when I have to speak in class.

(3) ______________ she couldn't change the assignment for me. But she did have some advice. (4) ______________ put off the assignment. Then (5) ______________ practice my presentation with a friend. (6) ______________ if I practiced my presentation ahead of time, I would feel more comfortable on the day I actually had to give it. So, I hope Rita can come over tomorrow and listen to my presentation. Are you reading this, Rita? Please say "yes"!

COMMENTS (12) SHARE THIS

4 READING

A Read the article. Find the boldfaced words that match the definitions.

1. problems *pitfalls*
2. increase ______________
3. unclear ______________
4. concern for others ______________
5. talking too proudly about yourself ______________
6. not thinking you are better than others ______________

How nice of you to say so . . .

Everyone appreciates a compliment. They are expressions of admiration, acceptance, and affection that make the recipient of the compliment feel good and **boost** positive feelings in the giver of the compliment as well. Friendships and good working relationships alike can develop out of a well-worded and appropriately timed compliment. As in most areas of social interaction, though, giving and receiving compliments can present problems. What's meant to be positive can turn out to be offensive unless you're aware of the possible **pitfalls**.

One point that many of us forget – or perhaps never realized – is that the best compliments are specific. Instead of a quick "Good job!" to a colleague or classmate, mentioning how well organized their presentation was, or how it taught you something new, will have the greatest effect. Similarly, try to avoid **vague** language like, "Wow, you got a new haircut!" If the recipient of your intended compliment is feeling unsure about this new look, they might think: ". . . and it looks terrible!" Explain what's good about it or why it's an improvement so there is no misunderstanding.

Sincerity is also important when it comes to compliments. When salespeople tell you how great you look or how smart you seem, you can often tell if they really mean it or if they are just trying to get you to buy something. Similarly, other people, especially those close to us, can usually tell if a compliment is automatic or insincere. And a compliment that sounds forced can actually make the recipient feel worse than if we had said nothing at all.

How you receive a compliment can also determine if the exchange will be a positive or a negative one. Many people reject compliments by saying, "Oh, it was nothing," or "It wasn't me – Tom did all the work." This may seem like the right, and **humble**, thing to do. Accepting a compliment with no argument can feel like **boasting** to many people and in many cultures. However, in the U.S. and most Western cultures, graciously accepting a positive statement with a simple thank-you shows the other person that you respect their judgment and appreciate their **thoughtfulness**. So the next time someone comments on your new outfit, try to resist saying you bought it for next to nothing, it doesn't fit well and, anyway, your sister picked it out. Just smile, say thank you, and accept it as a positive moment for both of you.

B Read the article again. Choose the correct answers.

1. The author believes that giving compliments . . .
   - ☐ a. always has a positive effect.
   - ☐ b. can present problems.
   - ☐ c. isn't complicated.
2. According to the article, an unclear compliment . . .
   - ☐ a. is as good as a specific one.
   - ☐ b. always causes offense.
   - ☐ c. can be misunderstood.
3. According to the article, some salespeople might use compliments in order to . . .
   - ☐ a. make themselves feel better.
   - ☐ b. influence your decision.
   - ☐ c. appear humble.
4. In the U.S., rejecting a compliment gives the impression that . . .
   - ☐ a. you don't respect the giver.
   - ☐ b. you are boasting.
   - ☐ c. you feel insecure.

6 WHAT'S THE REAL STORY?

LESSON A ▶ *That's some story!*

1 GRAMMAR

Choose the sentences with grammatical mistakes. Rewrite them using the correct verb forms.

☑ 1. A government spokesperson has announced new economic policies yesterday.
A government spokesperson announced new economic policies yesterday.

☐ 2. Unusual weather events have been happening across the country.

____

☐ 3. Police arrested several identity thieves so far this year.

____

☐ 4. Burglars have stolen two paintings on Monday night.

____

☐ 5. Several observers saw a rare butterfly in Central Park over the past week.

____

☐ 6. Jazz pianist Jacqueline Gray gave a concert at the Civic Center last night.

____

☐ 7. The stock market has fallen sharply the other day.

____

2 GRAMMAR

Choose the verbs that best complete this update about an ongoing news story.

UPDATED 8:12 A.M.

The County Municipal Airport (1) *has delayed* / *has been delaying* a flight to London. The delay (2) *has occurred* / *has been occurring* because airline personnel (3) *have been trying* / *tried* to locate a snake inside the plane. While information is incomplete at this time, we do know a few things. As flight attendants were preparing for takeoff, several passengers saw a snake under their seats. The pilot alerted the flight control tower, and the flight was delayed in order to find the snake. Crew members (4) *have searched* / *have been searching* the plane ever since. They still (5) *haven't been locating* / *haven't located* the snake, and no one (6) *has come up* / *has been coming up* with an explanation as to how it got there. Technicians (7) *have removed* / *have been removing* a section of the cabin floor to see if it may have hidden there. All the passengers (8) *have left* / *have been leaving* the plane already. They (9) *have sat* / *have been sitting* inside the terminal enjoying free soft drinks and snacks.

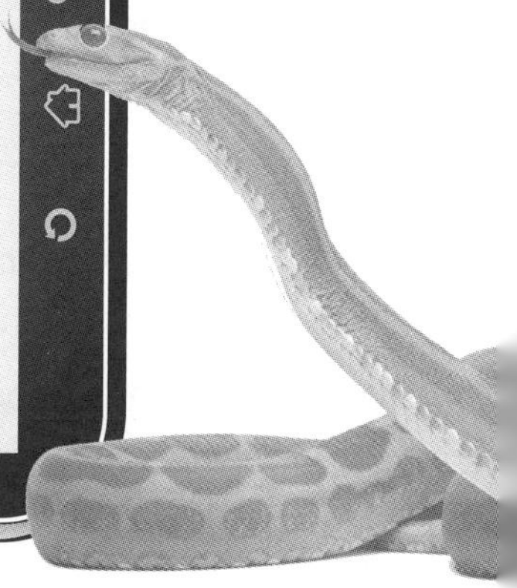

3 VOCABULARY

Match these headlines with the news events in the box.

epidemic	kidnapping	political crisis	recession	scandal
hijacking	natural disaster	rebellion	robbery	

Millions Found in Director's Secret Bank Account

1. *scandal*

$1.5 Million Stolen!

2. ____________

Airline Passengers Still Being Held Captive

3. ____________

Earthquake Destroys Houses Downtown

4. ____________

Prime Minister Resigns!

5. ____________

Virus Sickens Thousands

6. ____________

Hundreds of Inmates Take Over Prison

7. ____________

Millionaire's Wife Held for Ransom

8. ____________

Stocks and Employment Numbers Fall

9. ____________

4 GRAMMAR

Complete these sentences about some of the headlines above with your own ideas. Use the present perfect or present perfect continuous form of the verbs in parentheses.

1. Officials say the director (withdraw) *has been withdrawing hundreds of thousands of dollars from the company account for the past three years.*
   The director (deny) *has denied stealing any money.*
2. A bank robber (steal) ____________
   The bank robber (hide) ____________
3. Passengers on Flight 200 (hold) ____________
   The hijackers (demand) ____________
4. The earthquake (destroy) ____________
   Many people (volunteer) ____________

5 WRITING

A Read the news story. Then number the pictures in the correct order.

a. 4

b. ☐

c. ☐

d. ☐

Trapped Cat Rescued

After spending 14 days trapped inside the walls of a 157-year-old building in New York City last April, Molly briefly became a world-famous cat. Attempting to save the black cat, rescuers set traps and used special cameras and a raw fish to try to lure Molly out from between the walls. They even tried using kittens to appeal to the cat's motherly side so she would come out, but Molly would not budge. Finally, after they removed bricks and drilled holes into the walls, someone was able to pull the curious cat out of the tiny space.

The bricks have now been replaced, but Molly has been getting visits from tourists daily since she was rescued. Even so, Molly's adventures may not be over. Her owners say that at least once they have caught her looking inside a similar hole in the building.

B Read the story again. Underline the present perfect and present perfect continuous verbs.

C Write a news story about an interesting recent event. Use the present perfect, present perfect continuous, and simple past.

____

____

____

____

____

____

____

LESSON B ► *Storytelling*

1 GRAMMAR

Choose the correct expressions to complete the sentences.

1. She was amazed when she won the competition. *The moment / The next day / Until that time*, she had never won anything.
2. I felt awful about breaking my friend's phone. *Afterwards / When / Until that time*, I offered to replace it.
3. Despite my fear, I loved flying. *The moment / Up until then / Later*, I had never been on an airplane.
4. On Saturday, my mother left an urgent message on my voice mail. *Until that time / Later / As soon as* I got it, I called her back.
5. I had a delicious meal at a restaurant on Sunday. *The next day / When / Up until then*, however, I woke up with a serious case of food poisoning.
6. When I walked into the room, everyone yelled "Happy birthday!" *As soon as / Before that / Afterwards*, I'd never had a surprise party.
7. I got a big promotion at work. *Until that time / When / Later*, while I was telling my family, I felt really proud.

2 GRAMMAR

Complete the sentences. Use the past perfect or the simple past of the verbs in parentheses.

1. I couldn't figure out why she looked so familiar. Later, I ___*realized*___ (realize) she was my sixth-grade teacher.
2. I knew it was the delivery person knocking on my door. As soon as I ____________ (open) the door, he ____________ (give) me a big package.
3. While hiking, we suddenly realized we were lost and didn't have a compass or GPS. Up until then, we ____________ (not be) worried.
4. I had never experienced anything so exciting. Until that time, my life ____________ (be) very uneventful.
5. I went to the airport and booked the next flight. Afterwards, I ____________ (wait) for the announcement to board the plane.
6. It was my first time running a marathon. When I ____________ (see) the finish line in front of me, I ____________ (feel) relieved.
7. I finally passed my driving test. The moment I ____________ (receive) my driver's license in the mail, I ____________ (begin) to dance.
8. My father was moved by the performance. Before that, I ____________ (never see) him cry.

3 VOCABULARY

Use the expressions from the boxes to complete the conversation.

it all started when	the next thing we knew	the thing you have to know is

Mia: Hi, Ben. I heard you and Luke got lost on your way to the big game.

Ben: Yeah. (1) *It all started when* we began singing along with this cool song.

Mia: What happened?

Ben: Well, we were having such a good time that, (2) ____________________, we'd missed the turn for the stadium.

Mia: How did you do that?

Ben: (3) ____________________, when I'm singing a song I really like, I don't pay attention to anything around me.

I forgot to mention that	meanwhile	the other thing was

Mia: So you were having such a good time you didn't notice you'd gone past your turn?

Ben: That's about right. (4) ____________________, we'd driven about 40 miles too far!

Mia: Forty miles? Wow!

Ben: And (5) ____________________, we ran out of gas.

Mia: You ran out of gas? On the highway?

Ben: No, not on the highway. (6) ____________________ we'd decided to take a shortcut.

I forgot to mention that	to make a long story short

Mia: Did you make it to the game?

Ben: Yes. But it took us about three hours to get there!

Mia: Are you kidding?

Ben: (7) ____________________ we also stopped for pizza.

Mia: Seriously?

Ben: Well, getting lost made us hungry! So, (8) ____________________, we only saw the last half hour of the game.

4 READING

A Read the anecdotes about strange weather events. Then write brief summaries.

Susan's strange weather event was ______________________________

____

Elena's strange weather event was ______________________________

____

WACKY Weather Stories

Last summer, I was working at home on a sunny day. For some reason, I had gone around to the front of the house to get something. As I did, I felt some drops on my face, which soon developed into a very heavy shower. A few seconds later, I went to the back of the house and realized that it was totally dry there. The shower was only at the front of the house and not at the back. I stood in the hallway and looked one way – pouring – and the other way – sunny and dry. After a few minutes, the downpour stopped entirely. Up until then, I'd never seen such strange weather.

— Susan, United States

One spring day, I was sitting in the living room of my farmhouse in Uruguay watching TV and having lunch. I had just finished eating and was about to get up from the sofa to take my plate to the kitchen when suddenly a ball of fire the size of a soccer ball flew through the open kitchen window. About two seconds later, it disappeared under the front door and there was a terrible smell in the air. The TV and many electrical outlets in the house were burned, and a huge crack opened up in the kitchen wall. I didn't know what had happened until someone told me that the house had been hit by a *centella*, which is the Spanish word for lightning bolt. It was terrifying!

— Elena, Uruguay

B Choose true or false. Then rewrite the false statements to make them true.

	True	False
1. It was already pouring when Susan went to the front of the house.	☐	☐
2. Susan witnessed two kinds of weather at the same time.	☐	☐
3. The rain soon spread to both sides of Susan's house.	☐	☐
4. The fireball caused actual damage to Elena's house.	☐	☐
5. Elena understood immediately what had happened.	☐	☐

7 THE INFORMATION AGE

LESSON A ▶ *A weird, wired world*

1 VOCABULARY

Use the words and phrases in the box to complete the sentences.

app	the cloud	podcasts	text
blog	download	spyware	virus

1. This ____*app*____ lets me find the lowest price for gasoline from my phone.
2. Do you have Wi-Fi here? I need to ________________ some files for work.
3. Now that I store everything in ________________, I can access my data from anywhere.
4. If your device is running really slowly, it probably has a ________________.
5. Cal writes opinion pieces about music and posts them on his ________________.
6. Even though I moved abroad, I still listen to ________________ of shows from my favorite hometown radio station online.
7. Many people find it's more convenient to ________________ than to talk to people on the phone.
8. Some programs use ________________ to gather private information without your knowledge.

2 GRAMMAR

One of the underlined words in each sentence is a mistake. Circle it and write the correct word in the blank.

1. In the near future, more cars will been driven by computers than by people. ____*be*____
2. More tablets are being using in the classroom all the time. ____________
3. Medical data has going to be accessed online by both doctors and patients. ____________
4. More songs have be downloaded this year than ever before. ____________
5. All laptops in the store have being priced to sell quickly. ____________
6. More and more TV shows having been made available through apps. ____________
7. Increasingly, shopping and banking will be do on portable devices. ____________
8. Smartphones are going to been designed with even more features. ____________

3 VOCABULARY

Choose the connector that best completes each sentence.

1. Nat dropped his phone on the sidewalk yesterday. *Nevertheless* / *As a result*, it doesn't work anymore.
2. Parents should monitor the websites their children visit. *Additionally* / *On the other hand*, they need to talk to their children about Internet safety.
3. Cell phones are becoming more advanced. Some, *for instance* / *likewise*, have many of the capabilities of a computer.
4. Penny switched Internet service providers to save money. *Furthermore* / *In fact*, she's now spending $15 less each month.
5. I really don't like having a TV in my apartment. *Similarly* / *On the other hand*, it's useful to have one when I have friends over.
6. Higher education has become much more common due to technology. *For example* / *Therefore*, my cousin completed her degree online while living in another country.

4 GRAMMAR

Use the passive of the present continuous and your own information to complete the sentences.

1. Blogs *are being written by just about everybody these days!*
2. An increasing number of devices ______________________________
3. Many online classes ______________________________
4. Some spyware ______________________________
5. More and more apps ______________________________

5 WRITING

A Read the review of an online course. Underline and number the passages where the author of the review does the following things.

1. names and explains the service
2. explains where the service is offered
3. mentions positive features
4. suggests how it could be improved
5. states who would find it useful and why

http://blogs.cup.org/designbylila

Saturday, August 10

Curious about app creation?

KCC
CREATING MOBILE APPS

Creating Mobile Apps is an online course that gives students the chance to explore a variety of app-building programs, to learn about the various uses of apps, and to develop their own app. Offered by Kelly Community College, it's an excellent source of information and hands-on experience for beginners while providing exposure to the latest programs for those who already have some experience.

As someone already familiar with building apps, I was not very impressed with some of the material. However, I found the section on the possible uses of apps for everything – from shopping to home security – really eye-opening. Additionally, being able to create an app under the guidance of an expert made the whole process seem much simpler than expected. Overall, it provided a flexible learning experience, and I found that the biggest advantage of an online class is that you can move at your own pace. On the other hand, there's the obvious lack of real time spent with the instructor and fellow students.

I would definitely recommend this course to anyone looking to build an app. My only suggestion is that the college should offer better networking tools so that the discussions and brainstorming sessions are more efficient.

B Use one of these topics or your own idea to write a product or service review.

- a course you took
- a social networking site
- software you tried

LESSON B ▶ *Information overload*

1 VOCABULARY

Use the words and phrases in the box to complete the sentences.

banner ads	bumper sticker	infomercial	spam	text messages
billboard	crawl	pop-up ads	telemarketing	voice mail

1. Have you seen that funny ad for a tablet on a huge ___*billboard*___ on the highway?
2. A(n) ______________ is a long commercial that looks like a TV show.
3. I'm not sure how effective ______________ is. I never answer calls from numbers I don't recognize.
4. The ______________ at the bottom of the TV screen said a storm was coming.
5. If I don't answer my phone, just leave me a ______________.
6. I rarely see ______________ on my computer because my browser blocks them really well.
7. I find ______________ really annoying when they appear everywhere on a blog I'm reading.
8. All ______________ email I receive is sent to a separate folder that gets automatically cleared once a week.
9. I'm uncomfortable talking on my phone in public, so I prefer to send ______________.
10. The car in front of me had a ______________ that said, "I'm not driving too fast – I sure hope you aren't!"

2 GRAMMAR

Complete these negative questions or tag questions with *doesn't, don't, isn't, shouldn't,* or *wouldn't*.

1. ___*Don't*___ you think that there are lots of great cooking sites online?
2. ______________ it be terrific if Wi-Fi were free for everyone?
3. Sam's probably in a meeting. It's better to leave him a voice mail, ______________ it?
4. ______________ Sheila register for classes online before they fill up?
5. ______________ it seem like it's impossible to keep up with your social networking accounts at times?
6. Computer viruses are getting more sophisticated, ______________ you think?
7. ______________ it strange that no one has sent me any email today?
8. Banner ads get really annoying when they take up too much of the screen, ______________ they?

3 GRAMMAR

Rewrite the sentences in two ways using negative questions and tag questions and the words in parentheses.

1. It's amazing how much time someone can waste online. (isn't)

   Isn't it amazing how much time someone can waste online?

   It's amazing how much time someone can waste online, isn't it?

2. It would be great to get a bus wrap to advertise our business. (wouldn't)

   ____

   ____

3. Students should try to avoid sending text messages during class. (shouldn't)

   ____

   ____

4. It seems like new technologies are being invented every day. (doesn't)

   ____

   ____

5. It's annoying that some ads move all over the computer screen. (isn't)

   ____

   ____

6. It's amazing how some people can watch infomercials for hours. (don't you think)

   ____

   ____

4 GRAMMAR

Write negative questions or tag questions about things you can do online. Choose from the items in the box or use your own ideas.

shopping
reading the news
watching videos
planning a vacation
making new friends
looking for a job

1. *It's so convenient to shop online nowadays, isn't it?*
2. ______________________________
3. ______________________________
4. ______________________________
5. ______________________________
6. ______________________________

5 READING

A Read the blog post. Find the boldfaced words that match these definitions.

1. prepared; having no objection ___willing___
2. someone you know, but not well ____________
3. invited to connect on a social network ____________
4. accidents ____________
5. are grateful for ____________
6. at the same time ____________

Are You **Tech** Obsessed?

Tuesday, February 2

Most of us **appreciate** the convenience of our tech devices, but for some people, it goes beyond a healthy appreciation. Take this quiz about tech obsession. How many of these are true for you?

1. Do you ever have **mishaps** because you are using your device while walking?
2. Are you **willing** to wait in line for more than 12 hours to get the latest version of a device?
3. Do you wake up in the middle of the night to check all your social networking accounts?
4. Do you text your friends even when they are in the same room?
5. Do you ever watch different shows on your phone, tablet, and TV **simultaneously**?
6. Do you check your phone continuously when you're out with friends or family at a movie, a sporting event, or a restaurant?
7. Do you change your device covers all the time? Are you one of the millions who love choosing new "fashions" for their devices?
8. Do you use online slang when you're offline? For example, you might say about a new **acquaintance**, "I **friended** him in English class last week."

This quiz was pretty funny, don't you think? Unfortunately, I answered "yes" to seven of the questions! How about you? Are you tech obsessed like me?

Posted by Walker White at 5:36 p.m.

B Read the statements. Do you think the author of the blog post would say these behaviors are obsessive or not obsessive? Choose the correct answer.

	Obsessive	Not obsessive
1. You have to be reminded to check your device for calls and messages.	☐	☑
2. People don't always understand you because you use a lot of online slang.	☐	☐
3. You often trip and fall in the street because you're checking email on your phone.	☐	☐
4. You have been using the same version of your device for several years.	☐	☐
5. You have a huge collection of colorful covers for your devices.	☐	☐
6. You turn off your device when you're with friends.	☐	☐

8 PUTTING THE MIND TO WORK

LESSON A ► *Exploring creativity*

1 GRAMMAR

Rewrite the sentences by making the reduced clauses into full clauses.

1. A person with great cooking and business skills would make a good restaurant owner.
   A person who has great cooking and business skills would make a good restaurant owner.
2. Those able to think creatively are the best team leaders.
   ____
3. A person opening a new business should try unusual marketing methods.
   ____
4. People with musical skills should share their talent with others.
   ____
5. People hoping to succeed in the arts should be prepared for financial challenges.
   ____

2 GRAMMAR

Reduce each relative clause. Then complete the sentences with your own ideas.

1. A person who is living on a tight budget . . .
   A person living on a tight budget shouldn't eat out too often.
2. Anyone who is interested in becoming a doctor . . .
   ____
3. Someone who is considering an artistic career . . .
   ____
4. People who are able to work at home . . .
   ____
5. A supervisor who has too much work to do . . .
   ____
6. A person who is required to take a foreign language in school . . .
   ____
7. People who are becoming bored with their jobs . . .
   ____

3 VOCABULARY

A Write the nouns that relate to the adjectives.

1. curious *curiosity*
2. decisive ____________
3. determined ____________
4. disciplined ____________
5. innovative ____________
6. knowledgeable ____________
7. motivated ____________
8. original ____________
9. passionate ____________
10. patient ____________
11. perceptive ____________
12. resourceful ____________

B Now write sentences about these people using adjectives and nouns from above.

1. business executive *A knowledgeable person who has innovative ideas might make a good business executive.*
2. web designer ____________
3. journalist ____________
4. lawyer ____________

4 GRAMMAR

What qualities are needed to do these jobs? Use reduced relative clauses in your answers.

singer

1. *A person considering becoming a singer needs to be* ____________

landscaper

2. ____________

architect

3. ____________

5 WRITING

A Read Erica's story. Choose the word or words you would use to describe her.

☐ curious ☐ determined ☐ original ☐ resourceful

If you've ever planned a big event, something like this may have happened to you, but I certainly never thought it would happen to me! My fiancé and I were planning to get married in six months when his company decided to transfer him overseas – in two weeks! He wouldn't be able to return to the U.S. for some time, which meant we couldn't get married as planned. I told a friend about this, and she said, "So get married now!" I reminded her that there was no time to plan anything. She responded, "Then get creative." So I did. First, I designed and sent out email invitations. Then, as there was no time to book a venue, we decided to have both the ceremony and reception in my parents' backyard. My mother put together the decorations, which were flowering plants in pots. A friend of mine who's a chef prepared the food, and we had lots of cupcakes instead of a big cake. The clothes were the biggest challenge; there wasn't any time to make a new dress as I had planned. Luckily, I remembered the dress I'd made for a project in college. With a few alterations, it was perfect. I asked my three bridesmaids to wear dresses they already had – in any color. In the end, the wedding was fantastic thanks to everyone putting their creativity to work.

B Read the story again. Write a *P* where you think each new paragraph should begin.

C Write a three-paragraph composition about a problem you actually had or imagine you might have. How did you or would you solve the problem?

If you ____________________, something like this may have happened to you, but I certainly never thought it would happen to me. ____________________

____

____

____

____

____

____

____

____

____

LESSON B ► *Ideas that work*

1 VOCABULARY

Choose the word that best completes each sentence.

1. Seat belts alone did not protect car passengers enough, which is why researchers (*found*) / *made* / *solved* a safer solution: air bags for cars.
2. You need to *explore* / *organize* / *solve* your information before you present it to other people. Otherwise, they won't understand it.
3. Our report *explored* / *made* / *solved* several possibilities for increasing the car's efficiency.
4. The board of directors *analyzed* / *found* / *organized* the alternatives carefully when they chose a new location for the research facility.
5. It's important to consider many solutions when you are *making* / *organizing* / *solving* a problem.
6. Our science experiment didn't work. We *explored* / *made* / *solved* a mistake in the calculations.

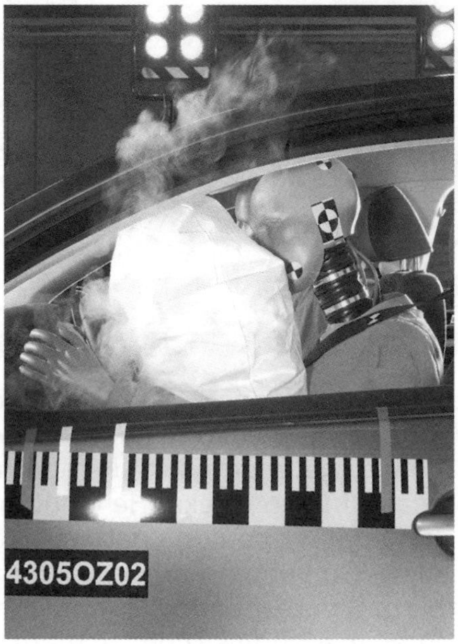

2 GRAMMAR

Read the conversation. Find the mistakes in the underlined sentences, and rewrite them so that they are correct. The mistake might be use of commas.

A: Why are we leaving so early? The meeting doesn't start for another 30 minutes!

B: At this time of day, the traffic is terrible! (1) It moves at only about 20 miles an hour, that means we need to leave now.

A: Why don't we take public transportation?

B: (2) The buses are even slower which is why people avoid using them.

A: Then how about walking? (3) The office is a short distance from here, which it means that it shouldn't take long.

B: True. (4) And we can get some exercise, too, it is great!

1. *It moves at only about 20 miles an hour, which means (that) we need to leave now.*
2. ______
3. ______
4. ______

3 GRAMMAR

Write sentences about these topics. Use non-defining relative clauses beginning with *which is why* or *which means (that).*

the common cold

ATM

video chatting

pollution

1. There is no cure for the common cold, *which is why researchers are working to find one.*
2. ATMs are available everywhere, ______________________________
3. Video chatting is easy for almost everyone, ______________________________
4. Pollution has become less of a problem in many cities, ______________________________

4 GRAMMAR

Combine the sentences with non-defining relative clauses beginning with *which is why, which means (that),* or *which is* + adjective.

1. People feel the need to keep in touch. Social networking sites are popular.
   People feel the need to keep in touch, which is why social networking sites are popular.
2. New diseases are being discovered all the time. Researchers have to work even harder.
   ____
3. Some people like listening to music on vinyl records. It's strange to me.
   ____
4. Traffic congestion is becoming a major problem in cities. New types of public transportation will have to be developed.
   ____
5. Reality TV shows are cheap and easy to produce. There are so many of them now.
   ____

5 READING

A Read the article quickly. Choose the best title for the article.

☐ Some People Will Never Be Creative ☐ How to Become an Artist

☐ What Everyday Creativity Means

When we think of creativity, we think of Mozart, Picasso, Einstein – people with a combination of talent and opportunity. But the truth is that all sorts of people are capable of engaging in creative processes. Just because you don't plan to be a famous actor or choreographer doesn't mean that you can't use your natural creativity and make your life your own masterpiece.

Zorana Ivcevic, a psychologist who studies creativity, has found that while some people fit into more traditional creative roles, as dancers or scientists, many others express their creativity through more routine acts. She also found that certain personality traits are shared by the "officially" creative and those who practice everyday creativity. Both groups tend to be open-minded and curious, and they are persistent, positive, energetic, and motivated by their chosen activities. And while 30 percent of the people studied showed no signs of creativity, they shouldn't lose hope. Other studies show that taking up creative pursuits actually makes people more flexible and less judgmental.

Experts at the Harvard Medical School define everyday creativity as expressions of originality and meaningfulness. Rebecca Whitlinger provided an example of this when she decided to make use of her seemingly useless collection of bridesmaid dresses. She resolved to wear them everywhere and asked friends to take snapshots of her wearing them in many unlikely situations, even while parasailing. Then it occurred to her to turn this idea into a fundraising event for a charity she worked for. Guests were asked to wear outfits they would be unable to wear again (such as a bridesmaid dress). Creative? Yes. Meaningful? Well, the fundraiser made $90,000 in its first few years.

"It's too bad that, when considering what endeavors may be creative, people immediately think of the arts," says Michele Root-Bernstein, co-author of *Sparks of Genius*. "It's the problem-solving processes they exhibit rather than the content or craft that make them so. Just about anything we do can be addressed in a creative manner, from housecleaning to personal hobbies to work."

B Read the article again. Choose the answers that best reflect the ideas in the article.

1. According to Zorana Ivcevic, how many people naturally show signs of creativity?
   ☐ a. everyone ☐ b. more people than most of us think ☐ c. very few people
2. According to the article, which of these personality traits is not as commonly linked to creativity?
   ☐ a. impatience ☐ b. optimism ☐ c. curiosity
3. Rebecca Whitlinger had the idea for a fundraising event when she . . .
   ☐ a. joined a charity. ☐ b. took up photography. ☐ c. creatively reused some clothes.
4. Michele Root-Bernstein believes that creativity can be . . .
   ☐ a. found in everything we do. ☐ b. found only in the arts. ☐ c. hard to define.

9 GENERALLY SPEAKING

LESSON A ► *How typical are you?*

1 GRAMMAR

Choose the expression that best completes each sentence.

1. *Unlike* / *While* many Americans, people in my country do not watch a lot of TV.
2. *In contrast to* / *While* many of my friends eat meat, I'm a vegetarian.
3. Monica is a typical teenager, *unlike* / *except for the fact that* she likes to get up early in the morning.
4. *Unlike* / *While* lots of my friends, I spend very little time on my phone.
5. I'm similar to people my age, *while* / *except that* I don't live at home.
6. *Unlike* / *While* most of my classmates, I prefer walking home to taking the bus.
7. Students in my country are just like other teens, *unlike* / *except that* we sometimes have to go to school on Saturdays.
8. I like all kinds of music, *except that* / *except for* jazz.

2 VOCABULARY

Use the words and phrases in the box to complete the sentences.

amenable
conform to
conservative
fits in
follows the crowd
make waves
rebellious
unconventional

1. Emma ___fits in___ easily with the other girls in her college.
2. I don't mind working overtime. I'm actually quite ________________ to it.
3. Neil likes to do his own thing. He doesn't ________________ other people's ideas.
4. Sam does the opposite of what people tell him to do. He's very ________________.
5. My town is very resistant to change. It's quite ________________.
6. Sadie always goes along with her friends' plans. She doesn't like to ________________.
7. Jake has ________________ ideas about his work. He tries to be original.
8. My cousin usually ________________ when it comes to fashion. She likes to dress exactly like her friends.

3 GRAMMAR

Read these descriptions of people. Who are you similar to or different from? Write sentences using *unlike, while, in contrast to, except that, except for,* and *except for the fact that.*

What are you like?

I am a college sophomore, and my major is English literature. My interests include tennis, reading, and travel. I enjoy exploring new places – especially places few people visit.

—KIM

Hi! I love music of all kinds, and I play guitar in a band. I love loud music – the louder the better. I'm interested in musical instruments, and I enjoy collecting them.

—MARIA

I am a 25-year-old computer science student. I am very interested in technology and soccer. I love building computers in my spare time.

—DONALD

Do you like visiting historical sites? Do you enjoy reading books about history? I do. I am 23 and an accountant, but my real passion is history. I also enjoy collecting rare coins.

—LUIS

1. *I have a lot in common with Kim, except that I don't like sports.*
2. ______________________________
3. ______________________________
4. ______________________________

4 WRITING

A Read these paragraphs and answer the questions.

More and more Americans are living alone nowadays. While an increasing number of people end up living alone because of varying life circumstances, such as a change in marital status, more people are choosing to live alone today than in the past. According to a recent U.S. census, 28 percent of all households in the United States are made up of just one person. This is a dramatic change from the extended families of just a couple of generations ago.

1. What is the topic sentence?

____

2. What reasons are given to support the topic sentence?

____

____

3. What fact is given to support the topic sentence?

____

The typical American living alone is neither old nor lonely. In fact, about 5 million people between the ages of 18 and 34 live alone, and the majority of them have chosen to do so. They are acting on a desire to be more independent, and they often have a more varied social life.

4. What is the topic sentence?

____

5. What fact is given to support the topic sentence?

____

6. What reasons are given to support the topic sentence?

____

____

B Choose the topic sentence below that you like best. Then add at least four supporting statements to make a complete paragraph.

- It is *unusual / typical* for young people in my country to live alone.
- It is *easy / difficult* to get into college in my country.

____

____

____

____

____

____

1 GRAMMAR

Complete the blog post with *used to* or *would* and the words in the box. Sometimes more than one answer is possible.

like	listen	not be	not turn on	play	save	watch

http://blogs.cup.org/ryansreflections

Sunday, March 14

I had a funny conversation with my grandfather the other day. He was telling me what things were like when he was a kid. First of all, there (1) ___*didn't use to be*___ any technology like tablets, smartphones, or handheld game consoles to entertain him. When he wanted to hear music, he (2) ________________ to the radio, or he (3) ________________ a record on a record player. He did have a TV, but he (4) ________________ it only at night. He (5) ________________ the TV during the day because there were only four channels, and the programs were boring in the daytime. He also said he (6) ________________ reading mystery and suspense novels. He (7) ________________ his allowance to buy his favorite books. I feel kind of bad for my granddad – it doesn't sound like the most exciting childhood.

2 VOCABULARY

Complete the conversation with *keep* or *stay.* Sometimes more than one answer is possible.

Lola: Mrs. Wu's class is so difficult! I'm always up late studying for her class, so I can barely (1) ___*stay*___ awake the next morning. I don't know how I'll survive the semester!

Max: Yeah, I remember how demanding Mrs. Wu can be. My best advice is to (2) ____________ up with the work you need to do each day. And don't procrastinate!

Lola: That's good advice. Her assignments are long and complicated. I always worry I won't be able to (3) ____________ my grades up in her class!

Max: Even though you're stressed out, try to (4) ____________ things in perspective. Also, if you let her know that you'll do what it takes to get good grades, maybe she'll help you (5) ____________ out of trouble.

Lola: That's a good idea. I'll talk to Mrs. Wu tomorrow. And I'll (6) ____________ in touch with you to let you know how things go.

3 GRAMMAR

Rewrite each sentence using the past habitual with *used to* or *would.* If there are two possibilities, write them both.

1. James was a very good chess player when he was younger.
   James used to be a very good chess player when he was younger.
2. In college, my friends and I studied for our tests together at the library.
   ____
3. I always asked my older sister for help with my science homework.
   ____
4. My English teacher didn't assign work over holidays or long weekends.
   ____
5. Rowan lived in an apartment near the university.
   ____
6. Carrie emailed her mom every day when she went away to school.
   ____

4 GRAMMAR

Complete the sentences with *used to* or *would* and information that is true for you.

1. Three years ago, I *used to* live *in a very noisy apartment on a noisy city street.*
2. Last summer, my friends and I ______________________________
3. When I was younger, I __________ go to ______________________________

4. A friend of mine __________ have trouble in __________ class because ______________________________
5. My favorite teacher was __________. He/She ______________________________
6. When I was first learning English, I ______________________________

5 READING

A Read the article quickly. What is Deirdre Barrett's main theory on dreaming?

____

YOUR **DREAMS** CAN HELP SOLVE YOUR DAY'S **PROBLEMS**

The slumbering mind might not seem like the best tool for critical thinking, but according to recent research, humans can actually solve problems while asleep. In fact, one purpose for dreaming may be to help us find solutions to puzzles that bother us while we're awake. Dreams are highly visual and often illogical, which makes them useful for the type of "out-of-the-box" thinking that some problem solving requires, explained Deirdre Barrett, a psychologist at Harvard University. Barrett's theory on dreaming boils down to this: Dreaming is really just thinking, but in a slightly different state from when our eyes are open.

Barrett has studied problem solving in dreams for more than 10 years and has documented many examples of the phenomenon in this time. In one experiment, Barrett asked college students to pick a homework problem to try to solve while sleeping. Students focused on the problem each night before they went to bed. At the end of a week, about half of the students had dreamed about the problem, and about a quarter had had a dream that contained the answer.

Having extensively reviewed scientific and historical literature for examples of problems solved in dreams, Barrett also found almost every type of problem being solved, from the mathematical to the artistic. Many were problems that required the individual to visualize something in his or her mind, such as an inventor picturing a new device. The other major category of problems solved included "ones where the conventional wisdom is just wrong about how to approach the problem," Barrett said. She added that dreams might have developed to be particularly good at allowing us to work out puzzles that fall into these two categories. "It's just extra thinking time," she stressed – though it's time that allows us to think in more flexible and creative ways.

B Read the article again. Are the statements true or false? Choose the correct answer. Then rewrite the false statements to make them true.

	True	False
1. The creative thinking associated with dreams makes them good for some types of problem solving. ______________________	☐	☐
2. Barrett has only recently begun studying dreams. ______________________	☐	☐
3. The students in Barrett's experiment all solved their problems while asleep. ______________________	☐	☐
4. According to Barrett, only certain kinds of problems can be solved while dreaming. ______________________	☐	☐
5. Inventors may find dreams particularly useful. ______________________	☐	☐

10 THE ART OF COMPLAINING

LESSON A ► *That really bugs me!*

1 GRAMMAR

Use the clauses in the box to complete the sentences.

how quickly the battery runs down	when my favorite show is interrupted by a news bulletin
people who make noise when they eat	who honk their horns all the time
waiting a long time to be seated	why people push in front of me in line
water dripping in the sink	

1. The thing that really bothers me at the dinner table is . . .
   The thing that really bothers me at the dinner table is people who make noise when they eat.
2. When I'm trying to sleep at night, something that irks me is . . .
3. One thing I can't understand in the supermarket is . . .
4. The thing that really irritates me when I go to a restaurant is . . .
5. Something I can't stand is drivers . . .
6. Something that bothers me about my new cell phone is . . .
7. When I'm watching TV, one thing that bugs me is . . .

2 GRAMMAR

Write sentences about things that irritate you. Use relative clauses and noun clauses, and your own ideas.

1. *The thing that bothers me at the dinner table is when people talk with their mouths full.*
2.
3.
4.

3 GRAMMAR

Use relative clauses and noun clauses to write about everyday annoyances in these places.

on the road

in the park

in the library

on the subway

1. *The thing that annoys me on the road is when other drivers follow too closely.*
2. ______________________________
3. ______________________________
4. ______________________________

4 VOCABULARY

Choose the word that best completes each sentence. Sometimes more than one answer is possible.

1. One thing that *drives* / *gets* / *makes* me down is when it rains on the weekend.
2. Something that *drives* / *gets* / *makes* me up the wall is when I have to wait on a long line to buy one or two items.
3. The thing that *drives* / *gets* / *makes* my blood boil is when my sister borrows my clothes.
4. One thing that *drives* / *gets* / *makes* me upset is when people are rude to store clerks for no reason.
5. The one thing that *drives* / *gets* / *makes* under my skin is when someone's cell phone rings during a movie or play.
6. When I'm talking to someone, the thing that *drives* / *gets* / *makes* on my nerves is when he or she keeps interrupting me.
7. My sister sending text messages during dinner *drives* / *gets* / *makes* me crazy.
8. One thing my brother does that *drives* / *gets* / *makes* me sick is when he leaves piles of dirty dishes in the kitchen sink.

5 WRITING

A Read the email complaining about a service. Number the four paragraphs in a logical order.

To: customerservice@bestgym.cup.com

Subject: Complaint about personal training service

To whom it may concern:

☐ My trainer, Dan, has not arrived on time for a single 6:00 a.m. session. The earliest he has arrived is 6:15, and several times he has come at 6:30. I am paying extra for his services, and I am certainly not getting my money's worth. Dan also tends to wander off while I am exercising, getting involved in conversations with other gym employees. My understanding was that he would carefully supervise my training, which he has not done.

☐ When I signed up for the program, the head trainer and I sat down, discussed my problems and needs, and drew up a plan, which was signed by both of us. This will show clearly what my expectations were in case you need to see this in writing. However, I hope it's clear by now that my needs have not been met.

☐ I would like you to assign me a new trainer or refund my fee for the personal training service. If you can't do this by next week, I will take my business to another gym.

☐ I am writing to complain about the personal trainer who was recently assigned to me at your gym. I signed up for six weeks of the intensive training program, including an individual fitness evaluation, and I am extremely dissatisfied.

Sincerely,
Elizabeth Smith
212-555-0199

B Use the numbers you wrote for the paragraphs above to answer these questions. In which paragraph does the writer . . .

a. explain the problem in detail? ____

b. explain what she wants? ____

c. describe the type of service clearly? ____

d. mention evidence of a service contract? ____

C Write an email complaining about a problem regarding a service or product you are not satisfied with.

To whom it may concern:

____

____

____

____

____

____

____

LESSON B ▶ *Let's do something about it!*

1 GRAMMAR

Write *S* for a simple indirect question and *C* for a complex indirect question.

S 1. I want to find out how to use less fat in my cooking.
____ 2. Why people aren't concerned about the crime rate is a mystery to me.
____ 3. I wonder if other people are concerned about the pollution problems in our city.
____ 4. The thing I don't get is why food prices are so high.
____ 5. One of my concerns is whether I will be able to afford a new car.
____ 6. I'd like to know if the weather will be nice this weekend.
____ 7. How some people can listen to such loud music is something I can't understand.
____ 8. I want to know when a cure for the common cold will be discovered.

2 GRAMMAR

Use the phrases in parentheses to rewrite the questions.

1. Why are the trains running so slowly? (. . . is a mystery to me.)
   Why the trains are running so slowly is a mystery to me.
2. Will there be cheaper health care for employees? (One of my concerns . . .)
   ____
3. Why do I get so much junk mail? (. . . is something I can't understand.)
   ____
4. How can you eat so much and not feel sick? (What I don't get . . .)
   ____
5. Who should I call if I don't get my passport on time? (I wonder . . .)
   ____
6. Will politicians do more to help the environment? (I'd like to know . . .)
   ____
7. Why don't people turn off their cell phones when they're at the movies? (. . . is beyond me.)
   ____
8. Why can't James get to work on time? (. . . is the thing that concerns me.)
   ____
9. Why do I get a cold every summer? (. . . is a mystery to me.)
   ____
10. Did someone use my tablet while I was out of the room? (I want to find out . . .)
   ____

3 VOCABULARY

Choose the word that best completes each sentence.

1. Lena was *infuriated* / *insulted* when she missed her flight due to the traffic jam.
2. John was very *irritated* / *saddened* to hear about the house that had been damaged by the storm.
3. Vicky was *depressed* / *mystified* when the forecast called for rain on her wedding day.
4. The players on the football team were *humiliated* / *insulted* when they lost the championship game by 22 points.
5. We were absolutely *demoralized* / *stunned* when we found out we had won the prize.
6. Chiang was totally *baffled* / *discouraged* when a complete stranger started talking to him as if they were old friends.
7. Joan was *enraged* / *discouraged* when she saw that someone had damaged her car and not even left a note for her.
8. June became pretty *insulted* / *annoyed* when her Wi-Fi kept disconnecting.

4 GRAMMAR

Write sentences about each urban problem below or about ideas of your own.

transportation	sanitation	parking

1. I don't know *why bus service is so infrequent. It's almost impossible to get to work on time.*
2. It's beyond me ______________________________
3. I wonder ______________________________
4. My big concern ______________________________

5 READING

A Read the article quickly. Write the number of each section next to its title.

_____ a. Understanding What Chronic Complainers Want

_____ b. Understanding What Chronic Complainers Don't Want

_____ c. Understanding How Chronic Complainers Think

The Survival Guide For Dealing With Chronic Complainers

*Optimists see a glass half full. Pessimists see a glass half empty. Chronic complainers see a glass that is slightly **chipped**, holding water that isn't cold enough, probably because it's tap water when they asked for bottled.*

The constant negativity of chronic complainers presents a challenge for those around them. Trying to remain positive and productive when there's a constant stream of complaints can try anyone's patience. And trying to be helpful will only **backfire**. So here are some essential tips to help those who deal with chronic complainers on a daily basis.

1 Despite the **gloom**, complainers don't see themselves as negative people. They see *the world* as negative and themselves as responding to the unfortunate circumstances of their lives.

Survival Tip #1 Never try to convince complainers that things are "not as bad" as they seem. This will only encourage them to come up with 10 additional **misfortunes** that might help you understand how terrible their lives actually are.

2 Chronic complainers are looking for sympathy and emotional **validation**. All they really want is for you to tell them that, yes, they've gotten a bad deal, and you feel their pain – just not as much as they do.

Survival Tip #2 The quickest way to get away from a complainer is to express sympathy and then change the subject. For example, "The printer jammed on you again? Sorry! I know it's hard, but I hope you can be a trooper because we really have to get back to work."

3 The idea that chronic complainers' lives are filled with tragedy is a big part of their **sense of identity**. Therefore, even good advice is a threat, because what complainers really want is for you to know they are suffering. They will often tell you why your solution won't work or might even become upset because you don't understand how unsolvable their problems are.

Survival Tip #3 You should avoid offering advice or solutions and stick to sympathy. However, there are situations where a problem is obviously very real. In this case, offer sympathy followed by brief but clear advice, and it will probably be accepted and appreciated.

B Read the article. Find the boldfaced word that matches each definition.

1. lack of hope *gloom*
2. bad things that happen ________
3. your idea of who you are ________
4. have the opposite effect to what was intended ________
5. damaged because a small piece has broken off ________
6. proof that something is true or real ________

11 VALUES

LESSON A ▶ *How honest are you?*

1 GRAMMAR

Complete the sentences with *even if, only if,* or *unless*.

1. I wouldn't interrupt a lesson ***unless*** I had an important question.
2. I would leave the scene of a car accident ____________ I knew for sure that no one was injured.
3. ____________ I were really hungry, I still wouldn't take food that wasn't mine.
4. I would ask my neighbors to be more quiet in the morning ____________ we had a good relationship.
5. I wouldn't ask to borrow a friend's phone ____________ I knew he or she wouldn't mind.
6. ____________ I didn't like my brother's new wife, I'd still be nice to her.

2 VOCABULARY

Choose the correct words to complete the sentences.

1. Steph won't mind if we rewrite parts of her article. She's very *(agreeable)* / *rational* to change.
2. It's *disapproving* / *unfair* that Mrs. Moore only blamed Lydia for the accident. Terry was responsible for the accident, too.
3. I'm sure Mark wasn't being *honest* / *irresponsible* when he said he liked my new shoes.
4. I can't believe Brianna wasn't fired from her job. Her *trustworthy* / *unscrupulous* business practices have cost this company thousands of dollars.
5. Min-hee is a good choice for club treasurer. She's good with money, and she's quite *unethical* / *responsible*.
6. In many places, it's *illegal* / *logical* to use a cell phone and drive at the same time.

3 GRAMMAR

Respond to what the first speaker says in each of these conversations.

1. A: If I found a friend's diary, I'd read it.
   B: Really? I wouldn't read it, even if *I were really curious, because diaries are supposed to be private.*

2. A: You should never give a friend your email password.
   B: I would give a friend my email password only if ______________________

3. A: If I heard someone spreading false information about a good friend, I wouldn't tell that friend about it.
   B: I wouldn't tell my friend about the false information unless ______________________

4. A: I would lend my best friend money if she needed it.
   B: I wouldn't lend my best friend a lot of money unless ______________________

4 GRAMMAR

How do you feel about these situations? Write sentences about them using *unless*, *only if*, or *even if*.

- recommending a friend's restaurant you don't consider very good
- lending money to someone you barely know
- giving fashion advice to a friend whose clothes you consider inappropriate
- saying you like a gift that you really don't like just to be nice

1. *I would never recommend a friend's restaurant that I don't consider very good unless I knew he/she was trying to improve it.*
2. ______________________
3. ______________________
4. ______________________

5 WRITING

A Read this composition and choose the best thesis statement.

- ☐ I am glad that I learned the importance of being responsible when I was young.
- ☐ I am thankful that I learned the importance of saving money when I was a child.
- ☐ I feel fortunate to have learned as a child how important family is.

_______________________________________ I grew up on a farm. My family had to care for the animals morning and evening, seven days a week. Even during school vacations and on weekends, there was work to be done, and each of my brothers and sisters had jobs that our parents depended on us to do.

For example, when I was 12, my parents entrusted me with the care of the young animals. That meant that if an animal was sick or injured, I had to take charge, giving the animal its medication and generally making sure it had a chance to get well. Most farmers had problems with their calves frequently getting sick. I was proud that my calves were usually healthy. That fact alone proved to me that I was doing a good job and making the right decisions.

Another way I learned responsibility is that, from the age of 12, I was paid for my work. Because I was working hard for my own money, I learned how to budget and save. When I was 14, I was able to buy a 10-speed bicycle with my savings. And because I demonstrated how responsible I was, by the time I was 16, my parents trusted me enough to help with the farm accounts.

In conclusion, being allowed to make important decisions and take charge of my own finances at an early age taught me what being responsible really means. Now, in my working life, I know that if I take care of the jobs that are given to me, my colleagues will see they can trust me with even more challenging tasks in the future.

B Now write a composition about something you learned as a child that is useful to you now. Begin the paragraphs as indicated below.

I'm glad that I learned _______________________________________

____

____

For example, _______________________________________

____

____

Another way I learned _______________________________________

____

____

In conclusion, _______________________________________

____

____

LESSON B ▶ *Taking stock*

1 GRAMMAR

Complete the sentences with the correct form of the verbs in parentheses.

1. Jay: I'm taking a French class at the community college.
   Meryl: I wish I ___*had*___ (have) more time to learn a second language.

2. Diego: I have to study tonight.
   Jim: If you ________________ (study) yesterday, you would have been able to go to the concert with me tonight!

3. Camila: If only our neighbor ________________ (play) his music more softly at night!
   Derek: I know. I haven't had a good night's sleep since he moved in!

4. Rohan: Our boss is going to be upset when he sees what you've done.
   Julie: It's true. If I had been careful, I ________________ (not spill) my drink on my computer.

5. Albin: You look exhausted. Why don't you stop working for a few minutes?
   Lily: I wish I ________________ (take) a break, but I have too much to do!

6. Hiroto: I'm so glad you didn't get caught in that snowstorm!
   Kay: If you ________________ (not warn) me, I probably would have gotten stuck on the road.

2 GRAMMAR

Complete the sentences with wishes and regrets about the illustration. Use the phrases from the box.

forget my umbrella	check the weather forecast
wear my raincoat	find a taxi

1. I wish *I hadn't forgotten my umbrella.*
   ____

2. If only ________________________________
   ____

3. I wish ________________________________
   ____

4. If only ________________________________
   ____

3 VOCABULARY

Use the words in the box to complete the sentences.

compassionate	generous	resilient	selfish
discreet	indifference	respect	tolerance

1. Even though Mr. Soto gave a ___*generous*___ donation to the library fund, he wishes he could have given more.
2. If I had been more ________________, Jenny wouldn't have found out about her surprise birthday party.
3. Make sure to be on time for your appointment with Ms. Benson. She doesn't have much ________________ for lateness.
4. We lost all ________________ for Ben when he lied about what happened to the computer.
5. I think it's important to teach children to be ________________ toward others.
6. Gina is pretty ________________. Even though she lost the singing competition, she'll be ready to sing again tomorrow.
7. ________________ to global warming really bothers me.
8. Brad is so ________________. He only thinks about how things affect him.

4 GRAMMAR

Read each situation. Then write one sentence with a wish about the present or future and one sentence with a regret about the past.

1. Tim stopped at a store to get a soda. He put his wallet down on the counter. When he went to pick it up, the wallet was gone! His ID and credit cards were in the wallet.
   Tim wishes he could find his wallet.
   If Tim hadn't set his wallet down, he wouldn't have lost his credit cards.
2. Laura had a 5:00 flight. She planned to take the 3:45 bus to the airport. Unfortunately, the bus was late. She missed her flight.
   ____
   ____
3. Charles was planning to study for four hours for his driver's test the next day. He went to the movies with his friend instead and studied for only 20 minutes. He failed the test.
   ____
   ____
4. Maxine quit going to college in her junior year. She planned to take one year off to travel and then go back to school. That was five years ago.
   ____
   ____

5 READING

A Read the article quickly. Decades ago, what was the assumption about how the Internet would affect people's honesty?

____

Internet On, Inhibitions Off:
Why We Tell All On The Net

It is now well known that people are generally accurate and (sometimes embarrassingly) honest about their personalities when profiling themselves on social networking sites. Patients are willing to be more open about psychiatric symptoms to an automated online doctor than a real one. Pollsters find that people give more honest answers to an online survey than to one conducted by phone.

But online honesty cuts both ways. Bloggers find that readers who comment on their posts are often harshly frank, but that these same rude critics become polite if contacted directly. . . .

Why is this? Why do we become more honest the less we have to face each other? Posing the question may make the answer seem obvious – that we feel uncomfortable about confessing to or challenging others when face to face with them – but that begs the question: Why? This is one of those cases where it is helpful to compare human beings with other species, to set our behavior in context.

In many monkeys and apes, face-to-face contact is essentially antagonistic. Staring is a threat. . . . Put two monkey strangers in a cage and they keep well apart, avoid eye contact, and generally do their utmost to avoid triggering a fight. Put two people in an elevator and the same thing happens. . . .

For many primates, face-to-face contact carries a threat. When we're online, we're essentially faceless. Deep in our psyches, the act of writing a furious online critique of someone's views does not feel like a confrontation, whereas telling them the same thing over the phone or face to face does. All the cues are missing that would warn us not to risk a revenge attack by being too frank. . . .

Internet flaming and its benign equivalent, online honesty, are a surprise. Two decades ago, most people thought the anonymity of the online world would cause an epidemic of dishonesty, just as they thought it would lead to geeky social isolation. Then along came social networking, and the Internet not only turned social but became embarrassingly honest. . . .

B Read the article again. Choose the correct answers.

1. What do social networking sites and automated online doctors have in common?
   - ☐ a. They make people more honest.
   - ☐ b. They make people less trustworthy.
   - ☐ c. They make people more ethical.

2. A monkey that stands face-to-face with another monkey probably . . .
   - ☐ a. wants to be agreeable.
   - ☐ b. is showing respect.
   - ☐ c. is looking for a fight.

3. Why does the writer talk about monkeys and apes in the article?
   - ☐ a. To make a contrast with human behavior.
   - ☐ b. To help explain human behavior.
   - ☐ c. To point out animals are capable of dishonesty.

4. What does the author suggest is the cause of online frankness?
   - ☐ a. People have become less sociable.
   - ☐ b. It's human nature to confront others.
   - ☐ c. We don't feel threatened for saying what we think.

12 MOVING AROUND

LESSON A ▶ *Culture shock*

1 GRAMMAR

Look at the timeline that a mother has envisioned for her twins' lives. Are the sentences true or false? Choose the correct answer. Then rewrite the false sentences to make them true.

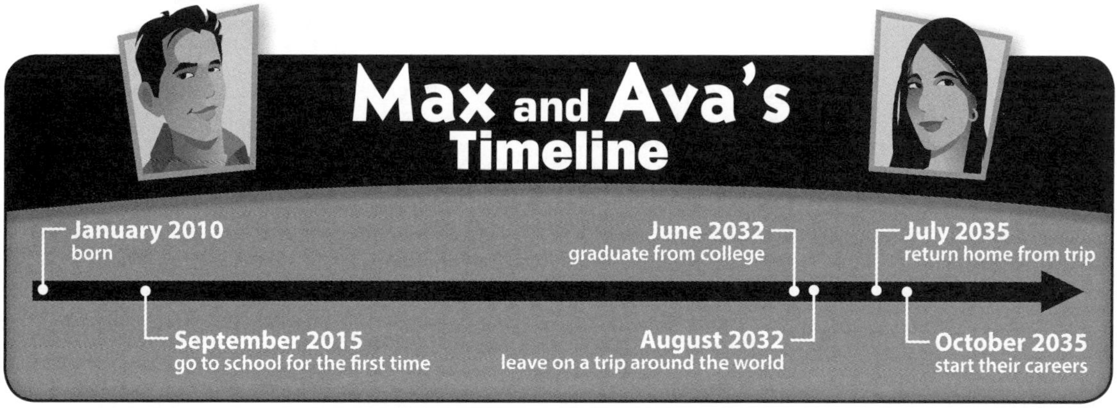

	True	False
1. By September 2026, Max and Ava will have been going to school for 10 years. *By September 2026, Max and Ava will have been going to school for 11 years.*	☐	☑
2. By July 2032, they will already have graduated from college.	☐	☐
3. By September 2033, they will be leaving on a trip around the world.	☐	☐
4. By August 2035, they will have been traveling for three years.	☐	☐
5. It's now October 2034. By this time next year, they will have started their careers.	☐	☐
6. By October 2037, they will have been working for one year.	☐	☐

2 GRAMMAR

Complete the email. Use the future perfect or future perfect continuous of the verbs in parentheses.

To: Julie
Cc:
Subject: Paris!

Hi Julie,

By this time tomorrow, I (1) ___*will have arrived*___ (arrive) in France! I can't believe I get to study there! I'm nervous, but I hope by next week I (2) ______________ (learn) my way around. I'm sure I (3) ______________ (get) lost several times by then, too.

I (4) ______________ (meet) my roommate by this time next week, too. I hope she's nice. I'm nervous about meeting my new classmates. They're all from different parts of the world. I hope in six month's time I (5) ______________ (have) the opportunity to get to know each of them.

I can't wait for you to visit. Maybe you can come in December. That should give you some time to save money since you (6) ______________ (work) for a few months by then. And also by then, I'm sure I (7) ______________ (find) some great restaurants to eat at. I know how much you love French food!

I already miss you, so write to me as soon as you can!

Isabella

3 VOCABULARY

Complete the sentences with *about*, *in*, *of*, *to*, or *with*. Sometimes more than one answer is possible.

1. Kenji can't wait for his trip to the United States. He's looking forward ___*to*___ visiting California and New York.
2. Before Nicole left to work in her company's branch in Spain, she participated ________ a special training program.
3. If you have the opportunity to work in another country, don't be scared ________ taking it.
4. Michelle made friends easily after she adjusted ________ the new culture.
5. Jack was very excited ________ meeting his colleagues from China.
6. If you want to take advantage ________ your school's study abroad programs, you should talk to your adviser.
7. She wasn't familiar ________ the customs in her host country, but she soon adapted to life there.
8. As soon as he became aware ________ his company's policy allowing employees to work in another country for a year, he decided to apply.

4 WRITING

A Read the three conclusions about the experience of working abroad. Write the letters of all the methods used in each conclusion.

a. looks to the future
b. concludes with the main idea
c. summarizes the main points
d. makes recommendations

b, c, d **1.** In conclusion, those who decide to live abroad gain experience of other cultures, understanding of others' work practices, and a deeper empathy for people of other countries. Working abroad widens your view of the world, and that will be of lasting benefit in both your work and personal life. Definitely do it if you can.

______ **2.** To sum up, people who decide to work abroad will have the opportunity to change their lives in several ways. First, they will develop a deep understanding of another culture. Second, they will gain first-hand experience of work practices that can give them a new perspective on their own work. Last, they will broaden their knowledge of the world in ways that will stay with them for the rest of their lives.

______ **3.** In brief, whether you decide to work abroad on a short-term basis or for an extended period, it is an experience that is educational, pleasurable, and practical. The experience allows you to flourish in all aspects of your life long after the experience is over and is highly recommended for anyone who has the chance to do it.

B Underline the words or phrases in each conclusion above that helped you decide which methods were used.

C Write a short essay about what people should expect to experience if they come to work or study in your country. Your conclusion should contain at least one of the methods listed above.

1 GRAMMAR

Use the verbs in parentheses to complete the email. Use mixed conditionals.

Dear Elena,

Well, I'm halfway through my tour of Peru. I'd like to say that everything is going well, but unfortunately, that isn't the case. I think if I (1) ***had prepared*** (prepare) a little more thoroughly, I (2) ____________________ (enjoy) myself a lot more right now. I guess if I (3) ____________________ (take) more time to research where I was going to stay, I (4) ____________________ (have) a better time in this beautiful country.

My biggest mistake is that I didn't bring the right clothes. I brought all my summer clothes, and it is absolutely freezing! If I (5) ____________________ (bring) the right clothes, I (6) ____________________ (feel) more comfortable right now. Instead, I've been staying indoors as much as possible and have a terrible cold. I went to a local pharmacy to get some cold medicine, but I had some trouble reading the labels. I think I bought the wrong medicine. If I (7) ____________________ (buy) the right medicine, I (8) ____________________ (not sneeze) all the time! If I (9) ____________________ (follow) your advice about the weather and accommodations, I (10)____________________ (not have) so many problems right now!

Anyway, I'll remember next time.
I miss you!

Love,
Sophia
Attached: perutrip014.jpg

2 GRAMMAR

Match the clauses to make conditional sentences. Write the correct letter.

1. If I had packed more carefully, _____
2. If I hadn't chosen a discount airline, _____
3. If I had studied English more often, _____
4. If I had left for the airport earlier, _____
5. If I hadn't forgotten my novel, _____

a. I wouldn't be afraid to ask people for directions.
b. I wouldn't be reading a boring magazine right now.
c. I wouldn't be searching my bags for my passport.
d. I would have a free movie to look forward to on board.
e. I wouldn't be worried about missing my flight!

3 VOCABULARY

What characteristics do you think would be most important for these people? Write sentences about each picture using the adjectives from the box.

culturally aware	nonconforming	open-minded	self-motivated
culturally sensitive	nonjudgmental	self-assured	self-reliant

mountain climber

businessperson abroad

1. The mountain climber has to be *self-reliant* because *she could be left on her own in an emergency.*
2. If the mountain climber weren't ________________, she ________________
3. The businessperson abroad should be ________________
4. If the businessperson abroad weren't ________________

4 GRAMMAR

Complete the sentences so they are true for you.

1. If I had been open-minded about *studying abroad in college, I would have much more international experience on my résumé.*
2. If I had been more self-assured when ________________, I ________________
3. If I had been more culturally aware when I was younger, I ________________
4. If I hadn't been open-minded about ________________, I ________________

5 READING

A Read the article quickly. Choose the tips that are mentioned.

- ☐ call your friends at home
- ☐ take a course in anthropology
- ☐ take a class for people going abroad
- ☐ spend a lot of time alone
- ☐ prepare for culture shock
- ☐ visit a doctor regularly

BEATING CULTURE SHOCK

You have a chance to live and work overseas, to get to know another culture from the inside. It's a wonderful opportunity, but don't be surprised if you experience at least some culture shock. "When you're put into a new culture, even simple things will throw you. You become like a child again, unable to handle everyday life without help," says L. Robert Kohls, an expert on culture shock.

Taking an intercultural studies or anthropology course at a university or attending one of the many classes offered for people going abroad is an important way to reduce the stress of culture shock, says Elsie Purnell, the founder of a counseling agency. She advises people going overseas to expect culture shock and to try to be prepared for it.

Someone living in a new culture typically goes through four stages of adjustment. Initial euphoria, or the honeymoon stage, is characterized by high expectations, a focus on similarities in the new culture, and a tendency to attach positive values to any differences that are noticed.

Culture shock, the second stage, begins very suddenly. The symptoms of culture shock include homesickness, feelings of anxiety, depression, fatigue, and inadequacy. Some people going through culture shock try to withdraw from the new culture, spending most of their free time reading about home, sleeping 12 hours a night, and associating only with others from their own country. Others eat too much, feel irritable, and display hostility or even aggression.

A period of gradual adjustment is the third stage. Once you realize you're adjusting, life gets more hopeful. "You've been watching what's been going on, interpreting things, and you're starting to recognize the patterns and learn the underlying values of the culture," says Kohls. It feels more natural, and you feel more self-assured.

The fourth stage, full adjustment, can take several years, and not everyone achieves it. According to Kohls, a lot depends on people's personalities – how rigid or how easygoing they are – and how seriously they try to understand the new culture.

B Read the article again. At what stage would someone make the following statements?

	Stage 1	Stage 2	Stage 3	Stage 4
1. "I just want to sleep all the time."	☐	☑	☐	☐
2. "The customs here are different, but they are so wonderful and sophisticated!"	☐	☐	☐	☐
3. "I've lived here for so many years that it feels like home."	☐	☐	☐	☐
4. "Everyone has been so helpful and friendly since I've arrived. The people here are so polite!"	☐	☐	☐	☐
5. "I'm starting to understand the culture and feel more self-assured here."	☐	☐	☐	☐
6. "I only spend time with people from my own country."	☐	☐	☐	☐